Parenting in the '90s ®
A Comprehensive Resource Guide
for Austin Parents

by Xochitl Aguilar, Age 11, Zilker Elementary

Parenting in the '90s ®

A Comprehensive Resource Guide for Austin Parents

Edited by
Sandy J. Kemp

CAMERON
PUBLICATIONS

AUSTIN, TEXAS

Published by Cameron Publciations
P.O. Box 3493
Austin, Texas 78764
512-442-7979

The opinions expressed by the authors of the articles and by the profiled businesses are not necessarily the opinions of the publisher.

Quotations in the book were used with permission from the following sources:
Kahlil Gibran, *The Prophet*. Copyright © 1923 by Alfred A. Knopf. *Great Occasions: Readings for the Celebrationof Birth, Coming of Age, Marriage and Death*, edited by Carl Seaburg. Copyright © by Beacon Press 1968.

Publisher's Cataloging-in-Publication Data
Kemp, Sandy J., 1952-
  Parenting in the '90s®: A Comprehensive Resource
  Guide for Austin Parents
  1. Parenting—United Sates. 2. Austin, Texas Resources
  I. Title.
HQ755.8.K45   1990   649'.1   89-25170
ISBN 0-9624402-0-5

A BARD PRODUCTIONS BOOK
Writing and copy editing: Judy Barrett Spurgin
Cover Design: Suzanne Pustejovsky
Text design: Bob Helberg
Proofreading: Lynne Loomis
Composition and production:
        Art Marketing Services, Georgetown, Texas

TABLE OF CONTENTS

PARENTING IN THE '90s . . . . We're lucky these days to have so much information and so many resources available to help make our parenting easier and more effective. Finding the information, however, is often a job in itself.

That's where this book comes in handy. I carefully selected local professionals to write 41 educational and informative parenting articles on topics addressing parental concerns about children from infancy through adolescence. Chapters I through V focus on different age groups. Chapter VI gives you valuable information about "Adding to The Family." Chapter VII is devoted to "Special Situations," and Chapter VIII includes city, county, and state resources.

To help you in selecting services for your family, each chapter has a profile section which gives you a more personalized view of exactly what services are offered. Each of these businesses was chosen and interviewed by a parent who asked the questions to which most parents want answers. The profiles were paid for by the businesses to help produce and distribute this book to the community. You can make your own decisions as to whether the services offered will meet your needs by reading the profiles and visiting the businesses.

Sandy J. Kemp
Editor & Publisher

The mother of a three-year-old son, Ms. Kemp has learned firsthand the importance and value of parent education. She has researched and authored papers on topics ranging from the effects of television advertising on children's nutritional attitudes to female entrepreneurship. She has been an Austin resident for 12 years.

by Cameron Kemp, age 2-1/2, First Baptist Mother's Day Out

I want personally to thank everyone who was committed to and involved in making this book a reality. In particular:

• Glenn Wood, M.D., Pediatrician, for helping me to put my original ideas into words.
• Ray Bard, Consultant and Director of Production.
• Judy Barrett Spurgin, Copy Editor, Writer, Composition.
• Bob Helberg, Text Design and Layout.
• Suzanne Pustejovsky, Cover Design.
• Lynne Loomis, Proofreading.
• Jane Steig Parsons of Prints Charming Photography for cover photos.
• Mary Wasmuth of About Images for photos of the children's art work from the public schools.
• Daniel Schaefer of Schaefer Photography for photos of the children's art work from the private schools.
• All the children whose art works grace these pages and their teachers from public and private schools who cooperated in collecting the art.
• All the professionals who contributed their knowledge, expertise, and insight.
• Monica Folk and Linda Lee for their help in researching and interviewing businesses for the profile sections.

And most of all, thanks to my family for their inspiration, encouragement, and patience:
• My dad, Bernardo, for showing me the entrepreneurial path.
• My mom, Terry, for teaching me that I can do anything, and for serving as "Gal Friday" for this project.
• My son, Cameron, to whom this book is dedicated.

CHAPTER I

Joys of Infancy
(0-1 years)

by Kristie Pannell, Grade 6, O. Henry Middle School

Caring for the Newborn

by Glenn G. Wood, M.D.

As you read this, you are probably resting after the delivery of your new baby. Perhaps you feel both relieved that the baby is here and nervous about caring for your new child. These first days are important for both of you, as parents, to begin experiencing your new baby. You will be given many suggestions from many people in the weeks to come, but you should not be afraid to use your own common sense. Each infant is unique, and so appropriate care varies slightly for each baby. Parenting is a combined effort. You should both be involved in your baby's well-being, which includes playtime, feedings, changing, baths, and general care. Close contact with both mother and father gives the baby the greatest benefit. As first-time parents, you may be nervous about holding your tiny baby; however, babies are durable and enjoy being held, cuddled, talked and sung to, rocked, and loved.

COMFORT

A comfortable temperature, without drafts, is recommended. Do not over-dress your baby in summer, but in winter, footed pajamas keep the baby from becoming chilled. Your baby should have its own bed with no pillow and, if possible, should sleep in a separate room.

FEEDING

This is an excellent time to experience closeness with your new baby. Eye contact and talking are important while you feed your baby.

Feeding schedules should be flexible. Initially, it is best to feed your baby as often as he or she is hungry. It is difficult to overfeed a baby. Some babies confuse their nights and days and feed more often at night. In those cases it is best to gently waken the baby after three to four hours in the day and feed him or her to decrease the night feedings. Babies get plenty of water in the milk, so additional water is not usually needed.

The amount taken and the interval between feedings will increase as your baby gets older. He or she should be burped by placing the baby over your lap or shoulder and gently rubbing or patting the back. Most babies will spit up at times, and this should not concern you. After feeding, your baby will usually sleep, and he or she should be laid down on the abdomen to avoid aspiration in case of spitting up.

BREASTFEEDING

Successful breastfeeding involves three concerns:

1. Fluids and nutrition—Your baby takes lots of water and calories from the mother. Therefore, it is important that you drink plenty of liquids and eat a well-balanced diet. You should also continue your prenatal vitamins. Alcohol, cigarettes, and laxatives should be limited. No drug should be taken without first discussing its use with your physician.

2. Stimulation of milk production—The more your baby nurses, the more milk you will produce. By three to four months your baby will be taking double the initial volume of milk. Formula supplements should be used with care; they tend

to fill your baby, causing him to nurse less and you to produce less milk.

3. Relaxation while nursing—If you are anxious because it is your first time to nurse or because there is a lot of activity going on around you when you feed your baby, your milk may not flow as freely. This should be an unhurried time of pleasure for both you and your baby.

Your nipples should be cleansed with a moistened cloth before and after breastfeeding. Gently blot dry. A nursing bra and pads should be used, and the pads should be kept dry. If tenderness occurs, it is important to continue nursing or expressing milk since engorgement may lead to mastitis or breast infection. Your baby should begin nursing on the same side he or she finished on at the last feeding. Once nursing is well established, do not feed more often than every two hours.

FORMULA FEEDING

There are many good formulas available. Originally one without extra iron may be used, but by two months, formula with iron should be used. The formulas come in ready-to-feed, concentrate, and powder forms. Follow the directions carefully. The powder is the least expensive. If water is added, it need not be sterilized if a city supply of water is used. Once water is added, the milk should be refrigerated and used within one to two days. The milk should be warmed before feeding and tested by dropping on the inside of your wrist. All utensils used in feeding, including bottles, measuring pitchers, and can openers, should be washed frequently.

GENERAL CARE

Do not immerse your baby in water to bathe until the cord has healed. Until then, wash the baby with warm water and gentle soap. Cradle cap may be prevented by shampooing two to three times a week. Some dry skin is normal, and most babies will have a rash on the face and chest at first.

You should have no visitors for the first few days. This allows you and your baby to get to know each other and to adjust to the new situation. No one who is ill should see the baby no matter how minor the illness, and outings to crowded places should be discouraged for several weeks.

Glenn G. Wood, M.D., is a Diplomate of American Board of Pediatrics and Fellow of American Academy of Pediatrics.

by Rebekah Koeninger, age 4-1/2, Lake Austin Montessori

Making the Transition from a Couple to a Family

by Steven McAllister, CADAC

I have been counseling couples and families for more than 15 years, but what really qualifies me to present this information to you is that I am very happily married and have survived two children, so far. We have two daughters, a 12 year old and a three year old. With the help of my wife, I still have a pretty good recall of what it was like during those early years.

First I would like to present some basic characteristics of a good, healthy marriage:

1. Open and honest communication
2. Intimacy and nurturing, ie., emotional trust
3. Willingness of both partners to resolve conflict
4. Experiencing fun and passion
5. Active peer support, ie., relating with other individuals and couples
6. Willingness to face and deal with each of their own issues

Of course being in love with one another is very important, but I am hoping that the necessary love to carry you through is a given in your case. Don't worry if you and your spouse don't have all these characteristics moving in a positive direction all at the same time. The priority is to adopt workable goals for your marriage and to work toward them together, "one day at a time."

God certainly had the parents in mind, as well as the child, when he gave us nine months to become prepared. But is there anyone who really felt prepared for parenthood? I certainly thought right after the Lamaze classes that I was ready for anything. I can also remember the embarrassing statement that I made at that same period: "Parenting can't be all that tough. I bet it won't change things much at all around our house." I would like to publicly thank all the parents who just smiled as I spouted off that statement, and most of all for not coming to my house at three in the morning as I was walking the baby and asking me if I would like to repeat that statement.

The transitional period from a marriage to becoming a family is probably one of the most difficult times that a couple may ever know. I say this not to scare you, but to inform you of the possible stress that you may experience. Often when I am evaluating a couple in counseling, it is most often in this initial transitional period that the couple first lost connection with one another. It is not uncommon to lose that emotional connection. What does become unhealthy or destructive to the marriage is not recognizing the new stress that has entered the relationship and not doing something about it.

Here are some commonly experienced problems and some solutions that might be of help to you in your first few years of family life:

1. "My spouse and I never seem to have any time alone together anymore." You have to *make* time to go out together and have fun. This will be difficult at first, but you should try to set aside two time periods a week for just the two of you to spend time together. You may start by doing some of the things that you both enjoyed before you had a child.

2. "My spouse hardly ever wants to have sex anymore." Begin by communi-

cating your needs to your partner. Sometimes sex is physically uncomfortable for the woman right after giving birth. Give yourselves time in this matter; sex drives and opportunities will return after the birth of your child.

3. "My wife seems always to be busy with the baby, not giving me the attention she once did." This is a common complaint. The baby, as well as the mother, needs to form a powerful bond that is most intense in the first three years, and this bonding is often threatening to the father. Husbands need to communicate their needs; grieve the loss that you feel and don't give up. This period will not last forever, and your wife will return to you.

4. "My husband seems to work a lot more now, and when he is home, he seems to be unattached from the baby and me." Husbands need to resist the urge to check out emotionally through work, the home computer, or the TV. Both husband and wife need to communicate about their needs and identify things that they can do and enjoy together.

5. "My spouse and I don't enjoy our friends that aren't parents as much as we once did. They don't seem to understand us, and we don't have much in common anymore." Couples without children probably aren't going to understand what you're experiencing with your child, but that doesn't mean they are no longer your friends. You can still find activities to share with your old friends that do not center around your child. You can also expand your social world to include other couples who do have children. It is important to share your experiences with other parents. If you don't know any, try calling some of your old Lamaze buddies or ask your pediatrician for some names of couples with children the same age as your child.

6. "My spouse and I don't seem to be as close as we were before the baby came." Families can be a source of strength. Often we see only the sacrifices that we are making and not the benefits. The same is true in your marriage. We compare the way it is now with the way it used to be, and we feel a great loss. That loss is real; it is not ever going to be the way it was again. The ultimate challenge that every marriage faces is making the necessary changes to grow. It is these challenges that strengthen the marriage and that form new levels of intimacy and joy.

Yes, you will have to make some modifications and adjustments—babysitters, sleepless nights, and less time together, just to name a few. Is it worth it? Yes. The changes that my wife and I have faced have been the most rewarding times of both our lives. God's greatest gift to couples is the gift of a child and the challenges that they face as a family together.

Steven McAllister is the founder and director of the Recovery Unlimited Treatment Center.

Pathways to Healthy Self-Esteem

by Michael J. Sliwa and Kay G. Hibbs

An important dimension of parenting is providing for your child's emotional well-being. Your child's developing self-image will direct actions chosen throughout his or her lifetime. Children's self-images dramatically impact their fate regarding success or failure, drug abuse, marriage and family relationships—literally who they are and what they will become.

What is your understanding of self-image?

As professional counselors, we see few parents who give much thought to the role self-image plays in their children's development. It is our experience that, unless there is a family crisis, most clients, personal friends, acquaintances, and even professional colleagues rarely take time to consider how they think about themselves or the degree to which they feel loving toward themselves.

While your child does not enter the world with a self-image, one is quickly learned. Your child looks to you and other authority figures as mirrors that reflect who he or she is. Mother and father begin teaching self-image from the first contact with baby. Infants detect their worth from your words, voice tone, touch, gestures, and expressions. They do not question the reflection, but absorb 100 percent of it as absolute truth about themselves.

Your young child does not possess the autonomy to stand back and rationalize, "Dad is upset about work so that's why he doesn't want to play with me," or "Mom's angry because she burned dinner." Children tend to see themselves as centers of the universe, controlling or causing the things that happen around them. Therefore, they interpret the situation as: "If Dad does not want to play with me, there must be something the matter with me," and "Mom's angry because I did something wrong."

The diamond as a model of self-image.

Our perception of the importance of self-image led to the development of a model of the human self-image. In this model, we picture self-image as a multi-faceted diamond. At the unseeable core of the diamond are criteria necessary to be an acceptable person.

The core of the diamond contains answers to the most fundamental questions about the self. Some are as follows: Is it O.K. to exist? Am I O.K. as a human being? How successful can I be? Must I be perfect, or can I make mistakes? Am I ultimately a failure? Is it O.K. to take risks, and what are the parameters? Is it O.K. to trust? Additionally, the one-to-one relationship with the Creator is in the core.

We as parents, along with other significant caretakers, teach our children the answers to these questions, beginning with our first contact with the child. Remember that infants are quite sensitive to their environment, and that includes you. Voice tone, touch, smell, and even your emotions and mood convey messages to your infant. Later, gestures, expressions, words, and your behavior (toward your child, interactive with your child, and modeling) get added to the list of teaching tools you utilize as a parent, whether or not you intend it to be so.

As your children develop, so do the facets of their self-image diamond. Facets involve image of self within roles. Early facets are male/female, brother/sister, son/daughter, friend, and student. Later facets include athlete, lover, spouse, parent, employee, manager, and professional. A facet's size and shape vary across a lifetime, determined through individual observations and reflections of significant figures.

Ultimately, each of us has a facet for every role that we play, even if the role is not currently active. For example, your classroom days may be over, but you probably still have an image of yourself as a student.

How your child feels about himself on core issues—how he or she might answer those earlier questions—affects every developing facet. And once those beliefs are part of the core, they tend to remain rather constant.

For instance, if a person learns to feel that he is basically a failure at the core, no matter how successful he may be in any of his roles (for example, his career), he will still feel like a failure deep inside. While core self-image can change, it often takes the help of a trained professional. Therefore, we urge you to focus your energy on helping your child develop a positive core self-image.

As a parent, you can minimize long-term misreadings by your child. Pay attention to what you teach through words, voice tone, touch, gestures, expressions, mood, emotions, and behavior. You may fool another adult by saying one thing and acting in an opposing way, but you seldom fool the most perceptive observers of all—children.

It is virtually impossible to model a positive self-image for your child if you do not have one yourself. It is a truism that you cannot give your child what you do not have. If there is a deficiency in your own self-image core, you will likely pass a form of that deficiency on to your child.

Self-images are repairable. Yours and your child's.

To help you take inventory of your self-image core, think about how often you are dissatisfied with yourself, how your parents made you feel as a youngster, and what expectations you have of yourself as a parent, spouse, or provider. Are you often unhappy? Do you forgive yourself for your imperfections? A bit of soul-searching can give you a pretty good idea of what your self-image is and how you might be passing that along to your child. Remember, you *can* learn how to change your own self-image, and you can help your child develop a positive self-image.

Michael Sliwa and Kay Hibbs are counselors associated with Central Texas Counseling & Family Therapy Center.

Finding Quality Child Care

by Lois Gamble

As a parent, one of the most important decisions you'll ever face is the choice of child care. Certain factors have been identified by researchers, parents, teachers, administrators, and policymakers as contributing positively to the growth and development of young children. These criteria are the core of the accreditation system of the National Academy of Early Childhood Programs, a division of the National Association for the Education of Young Children. Knowing what to look for in these areas will help you identify quality care for your child.

Interaction among staff and children is warm and personal in a quality program. The environment is filled with spontaneous laughter, pleasant conversation, and exclamations of excitement. Guidance is positive and addresses behavior, not the character of the child. Individual needs are considered and met by adults who hold and touch appropriately, speak respectfully, and interact at the child's eye level. Adults encourage and accept verbal expressions of feelings and guide children in the development of problem-solving skills. Expectations of self-help and social skills are appropriate to a child's development level.

The **curriculum** in a quality program provides for all areas of a child's development—physical, emotional, social, and cognitive. It provides for a range of interests and abilities, and reflects the knowledge that young children learn through play. The environment is prepared for active exploration and interaction with adults, other children, and materials. Children can choose from among a variety of activities and materials which are concrete, real, and relevant to their lives. The daily schedule is planned with a balance of alternating active/quiet times and indoor/outdoor experiences. Adults extend learning by asking open-ended questions or making suggestions that stimulate the child's thinking. Rote memorization, flash cards, and worksheets are inappropriate learning materials for young children.

The **staff-parent interaction** in a quality program is based on the concept that parents are the principal influence in a child's life. Parents are welcomed into the center at all times and are encouraged to be observers and contributors to the program. Written statements of philosophy and goals are given to parents and discussed so that parents can make an informed decision about arrangements for their child. The transition into the program is made easier for parents and child by a pre-enrollment visit, orientation, and/or a gradual introduction of the child to the center. Staff and parents communicate regarding child-rearing practices to minimize conflicts and confusion for children. A verbal or written system exists for showing day-to-day happenings that may affect children. Conferences are held to discuss children's progress, accomplishments, and difficulties at home and at the center. Changes in a child's physical or emotional state are reported regularly. Parents are informed about the center's program through regular newsletters, bulletin boards, frequent notes, telephone calls, and similar measures.

The quality of **staff** is the most important determinant of the quality of an early childhood program. Staff have training in child development and/or early childhood education, as well as appropriate personal characteristics for successfully working with young children. The chief administrative officer of the licensed quality child care program is an early childhood specialist and has training and/

or experience in business administration. Staff in a quality program are adequately oriented in program goals and philosophy, emergency health and safety procedures, special needs of children assigned to their care, and guidance and classroom management techniques. Staff are expected to participate in regular training opportunities to improve skills.

The **administration** affects all interactions within a program. Effective administration is efficient and gives attention to the needs and desires of children, parents, and staff. Benefits and written personnel policies are available for staff. Regular staff meetings are held for program planning. The director makes appropriate use of community resources (educational and social services). Budgets are projected for at least one year. Staffing is sufficient to meet the needs of and promote the physical, social, and cognitive development of children. Staffing patterns permit continuity of adults who work with young children. Smaller group sizes and larger numbers of staff to children are related to positive outcomes for children.

The **physical environment** (indoors and outdoors) is clean, safe, attractive, and spacious. Materials and equipment are age-appropriate and provide opportunities for exploration and learning. Space is arranged so children can work individually and together in small groups, as well as in a large group.

Provisions for the **health and safety** of young children is essential. Good quality programs comply with all state and local regulations, act to prevent illness and accidents, are prepared to deal with emergencies, and also educate children concerning health and safety practices. Staff are free from physical and psychological conditions that might adversely affect children's health. Children need to have the necessary immunizations as recommended for their age group. Records are maintained that include pertinent health history, contact information, and names of people authorized to call for the child. At least one staff member who is certified in emergency first aid and CPR is always in the center. Adequate first aid supplies are available. The center has a written policy specifying limitations on attendance of sick children. Provisions are made for safe arrival and departure of children. Children are under adult supervision at all times. The facility is cleaned and disinfected daily. Soiled diapers are disposed of or held for laundry in closed containers inaccessible to children. The diaper-changing surface is disinfected or disposed of after each change of a diaper.

Meals/snacks are planned to meet the nutritional requirements recommended by the United States Department of Agriculture in proportion to the amount of time the child is in the program each day. Menus are provided to parents. Feeding times and food consumption information for toddlers is available each day. Chairs, tables, and eating utensils are suitable for the size and developmental levels of the children. At least one adult sits with children during meals. Toddlers and preschoolers are encouraged to serve and feed themselves. Infants are held in an inclined position while bottle feeding.

A systematic **evaluation** of children's development is compiled as a basis for planning appropriate learning activities and for use in communication with parents. Parents and staff evaluate the program's effectiveness in meeting the needs of children and parents. Staff are evaluated at least annually.

Lois Gamble is director of the NAEYC accredited Hyde Park Baptist Child Development Center in Austin.

The Development of Communication Skills

by Martha McGlothlin

Communication development—the development of speech and language skills—begins when a child is an infant. The parents of the child are of critical importance to the child's progress, interacting with the child from the time of delivery through the entire developmental process. By the age of six months a baby is laughing and saying a few vowel sounds. He responds when an adult copies the infant's vocalizations. As the baby becomes more mobile and less dependent, between the ages of six and 12 months, the baby adds more and different sounds and responds when he hears "No."

Around the time he begins walking, about 12 months, the baby begins to say a few words, such as "mama" and "daddy." In addition to the words, he will also produce fairly long sequences of sounds, including both consonants and vowels, that sound like real words but are not. You, as a parent, will feel that if you could just understand what your child is trying to say, he would be telling you a lot.

During the period 12-18 months, the child adds more words that primarily relate to what he wants and sees, words like "more," "juice," "cookie," and "bye-bye." He will also follow short instructions, such as "Go get your blanket," and will point to familiar items when requested to do so.

Around 18 months a change will occur as the toddler begins to combine two words, saying things like "more juice" and "cookie gone now." He may also begin to ask questions, but not necessarily the way we do as adults. He may say one or two words, but it will sound like a question instead of a statement because his voice will rise at the end, so "Daddy?" could mean "Where's Daddy?" or "Is Daddy coming?" His question may be accompanied by a hand gesture or facial expression indicating that he is asking a question.

Changes continue to occur in the 18-24 month period, with the toddler's ability to talk and understand expanding at a rapid rate. He follows simple two-part instructions, such as "Go to your room and get your pajamas." More words and phrases are added to the child's vocabulary, and by the age of 30-36 months, the child is talking in sentences and is able to carry on a short conversation with adults. He may have difficulty producing some sounds that are late-developing sounds, such as "r" and "th." However, by the time a child is three years old, his speech should be clear enough for an adult to understand most of what the child says. He may have some errors in his sentence structure, like saying "drinked" for "drank" and "sitted" for "sat," but these types of errors are not unusual for a child this age. Another common occurrence for children this age is a repetition of the first word in a phrase or sentence. He first gains your attention, but then may repeat the first word to give himself additional seconds to organize or decide what he wants to say. The best thing for you to do if these word repetitions occur is just to accept the repetitions as usual. *Do not* call the child's attention to the repetitions by telling him to slow down or to think about what he is saying. Don't put additional pressure on the child by asking him to "perform" for relatives and friends. With most children the repetitions will disappear in a relatively short time as the child becomes more skilled at saying longer sentences and using a wider variety of words.

Hearing is crucial to the development of speech and language. In the Central Texas area a number of children experience ear infections, often beginning when the child is an infant, which can affect a child's development of speech and language skills. So, if your child has ear infections, watch his communication development carefully. You will also want to have your child's hearing tested by an audiologist, a person trained to test hearing. No child is too young to be tested—even infants can be tested.

When should you become concerned about your child's development of speech and language skills? What should you do if you are concerned? First you should locate a book or pamphlet that gives you general developmental guidelines in communication, such as those described above. If your child is more than six months delayed, according to the guidelines, talk with your pediatrician. If the child is reluctant to talk in front of the pediatrician, jot down some examples of the way your child says things, and take those examples with you when you talk with the pediatrician. Frequently, pediatricians do not have the opportunity to hear the child talk because the child becomes anxious in the doctor's office and "clams up." The pediatrician must rely on you to inform him about your child's communication skills.

If the child shows a significant delay, your pediatrician will likely refer you to a speech-language pathologist, a person trained in the development of speech and language skills, for an evaluation. Following the evaluation, a conference will be held with you to explain the results of the evaluation, and you will be given a written report of the test results and recommendations. If therapy is recommended, your child will probably be seen once or twice a week to assist him in developing his communication skills. Parents are crucial and integral parts of the therapy program. Remember, too, that identifying a problem early is important, so don't be afraid to ask questions and seek help. Trust your own instincts.

Martha McGlothlin is a speech-language pathologist and the director of the Austin Center for Speech, Language and Learning.

by Jennifer Parker, age 4, Hyde Park Baptist Child Development Center

Changes in Your Child's Posture

by Donna Stoffa and Ellen Corley, Licensed Physical Therapists

Perhaps you recall being told, as a child, to stand up or sit up straight. Perhaps, as new parents, you will soon be saying the same things to your child. The postural problems seen in adults often develop in the early phases of life. The quest for upright posture begins early on with infancy and continues throughout adulthood. The greatest and fastest postural changes occur in the first 18 months of life. There is some variation between children and when they master certain postural "milestones." Milestones are activities which children normally reach at certain ages. The ages given are approximate, and some leeway should be given for individuality. By knowing what to expect, early recognition of problems is possible and may reduce the chronic troubles adults have come to know.

During the first month, the infant assumes a posture of legs and arms bent. After six to eight weeks, the baby will begin to straighten his arms and legs, as well as begin arching his back. By three months of age, most babies can control their heads when pulled to sitting by their arms and lift their heads while lying on their stomachs. Around five months of age, babies will begin to straighten their arms and prop up while on their stomachs.

Around seven to eight months of age, the baby will be able to roll from front to back and vice versa. During the eighth month of life, most babies are able to sit up without support and begin to pull themselves up to a standing position. You should begin to see crawling between the ninth and tenth month. Additionally, most babies will begin walking along furniture or when held by both hands. Walking normally occurs around ages 12 to 15 months and is characterized by legs widely separated and arms held up during walking.

By the age of 18 months, most children should begin to run very well. During the second year, the child will have mastered running and be able to climb onto a chair. During the third year, the child will learn how to jump and climbing will become easier for him. By about age four, your child will be able to walk and carry a glass of water at the same time.

As your child reaches adolescence, there will again be rapid growth and sometimes postural changes. Many people assume poor posture is due to laziness. If you are constantly reminding your child to stand or sit up straight, your child may need the help of a professional. In fact, postural problems may be due to structural and/or developmental problems that are out of the child's control. Here are some easily identifiable signs that something is not quite right with your child's posture/skeletal development:

- Uneven shoulders/hips
- Pants/skirt hems that are constantly uneven
- Rounded shoulders, head forward posture (This commonly starts in children who are taller than the majority of kids their age, but can lead to chronic problems if allowed to continue.)
- Excessive or flat curve in the low back region (Excessive curve may be present with "hunchback" appearance.)
- "Angel wings" or shoulder blades that stick out

• "Scoliosis" (curvature of the spine) may show up as uneven shoulders/hips, ribs appearing larger on one side (either front or back), or shoulders not "square" with the hips. This is often best observed in a bathing suit during spring/summer.

If any of these conditions are found and do not correct with efforts by you, it is advisable to seek the attention of medical personnel. Asking the child to correct a problem which is beyond his control may lead to a low self-esteem and actually make the problem worse. Physical therapists are trained in identification of postural problems and treatment of the same, and can evaluate your child and determine if treatment would be helpful. If you decide to seek treatment for your child, a referral from a physician is needed; however, an evaluation can be performed without a referral. The evaluation is strictly a physical examination to determine if physical therapy is appropriate for your child's situation. In most cases, home exercises will be an important part of the total therapy. Remember, early detection and treatment of postural problems may prevent the development of future troubles.

Ellen Corley has been practicing physical therapy for nine years with an emphasis on spinal/postural problems. Donna Stoffa, a pediatric physical therapist, treats children, from infancy to early adulthood, with special needs.

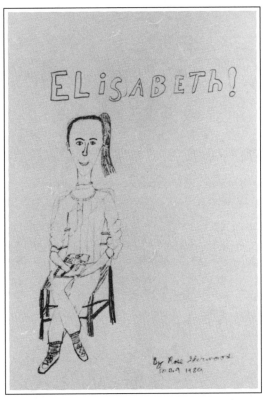

by Rose Sherwood, age 9, Austin Montessori School

Getting Mom Back in Shape
by William G. Franklin, M.D.

Well, the baby has finally arrived, and once the excitement of the birth has begun to fade, you may shift your gaze away from the baby to look at yourself. You may get quite a shock—the dreaded time to get back into shape has arrived. Your body may seem unrecognizable to you, and the sight of a large and flabby abdomen can be surprising and upsetting. A few lucky people deflate like balloons, but most don't, although everyone loses extra fluid during the first week.

REST

The postpartum period, the first six to eight weeks after childbirth, is a time of physical and emotional readjustment. Your body makes numerous physical adjustments in the first few days and weeks after childbirth. You may feel uplifted, or you may feel exhausted, but all new mothers feel tired and need rest. Adequate rest is essential to recovery. Try to rest an extra two hours each day. It takes at least three months for the body to readjust to its normal rhythms and longer if you are breastfeeding—so don't expect too much of yourself. Begin exercises when you feel you want to, never force yourself, and enjoy what you are doing. If you've had a Cesarean delivery, you'll need to take life particularly easy with extra rest and relaxation.

EXERCISE

During the first week after delivery, your exercise should concentrate on the abdomen and the pelvic floor. You should frequently perform the pelvic floor contraction exercises (Kegel) to encourage healing, reduce swelling, and restore the muscle tone in the pelvic floor. Gently tighten and then relax the muscles of your perineum two to five times each day. It is also time to begin abdominal tightening, but carefully as too much work will further weaken your pelvic floor. Don't worry about the size of your uterus; it will return to normal size within six weeks. You must be careful while doing abdominal exercises in case your stomach muscles have separated during childbirth. Try to exercise every day, but don't go for so long that you're exhausted; a little done often should be your goal. There are many abdominal exercises and many books that can describe these in detail.

In weeks two to thirteen, you will be ready to intensify, extend, and increase in number the variety of exercises you can do. Once you have practiced the postnatal routines regularly, you should try to include an activity like swimming, cycling, or brisk walking. You should begin these exercises in short, easy sessions and build up slowly as your stamina allows. Daily exercise is critical to getting back in shape, as is diet.

DIET

As you finish off the celebration champagne and consume the last of the coming-home cake, you begin to think about what to eat to return to your old self in a hurry. What you eat after your baby is here depends in part on whether you have chosen to breastfeed your infant. Breastfeeding requires an extra 500 calories per day—even more than the 300 extra calories required during pregnancy. If mom breastfeeds for three months, she will use up all her pregnancy fat stores even with an additional 500 calories of food each day.

It is very important that the breastfeeding mother not starve herself. This practice will reduce the milk supply. If you occasionally skip meals, you're the one who's likely to suffer. Producing milk, in and of itself, is a draining physiological experience. Add the strain of caring for a newborn without proper nutrition and the experience can be debilitating. Instead of starving, eat healthy food and make every bite count. Avoid foods that count for little but calories: cake, white bread, candy, pastries. All calories are not created equal. For example, the 1,490 calories of *one* typical fast-food meal (Big Mac, fries, chocolate shake, and apple pie), besides being loaded with saturated fats, excessive salt and sugar, and chemicals, are *not* nutritionally equal to the 1,490 calories in *two* well-balanced meals (tuna salad on whole wheat, cole slaw, skim milk, and one-half cantaloupe; veal chop, baked potato with sour cream, steamed broccoli, and slice of nature-sweetened apple pie). Your diet should be rich in high-nutrient, high-fiber, complex carbohydrates, such as whole grains, pastas, fruits, and vegetables. They are rich in vital vitamins, minerals, and trace metals. These principles hold true whether you are breastfeeding or not. In general, your diet should consist of three servings of protein, three servings of vegetables, one to two servings of fruits, four to five servings of complex carbohydrates, and one to two servings of fatty foods daily. You will also need to drink eight glasses of water each day.

For those not breastfeeding, the guidelines are still the same—you just don't need those additional 500 calories. Your body has gone through nine months of physical and emotional stress; good nutrition will not only speed your recovery, but also give you the energy to keep up with the demands of your baby. Don't go on a diet severely restricted in calories during the six-week postpartum period. Instead, cut down from your pregnancy intake sensibly, avoid empty calories, exercise religiously, and get plenty of iron supplementation.

Dr. Franklin is a family medicine specialist affiliated with Southwest Family Practice Associates.

by Shannon Bivens, age 5, Hyde Park Baptist Child Development Center

Planning for Your Financial Future
by Milton Hixson, CPA CFP

Financial planning is a process that requires a study of your individual goals, objectives, needs, and resources. This article is intended to provide basic planning steps which can be completed without the aid of an expert. You may prefer to use this article as a guide for the kind of advice an expert should provide.

Developing a plan

The first step in developing a financial plan is for you and your spouse to prepare a written list of goals and objectives. Each goal should be defined in terms of measurable dollars (today's dollar) and a time frame, and ranked in order of priority.

The next step is to gather information and prepare a net-worth statement (a snapshot of your assets and liabilities at that particular time), a cash-flow or income statement, and a budget of expenditures. Remember, you cannot effectively plan where you are going without knowing from where you are starting. Because most families will have difficulty in preparing the cash-flow statement, I suggest that for a three-month period you keep records adequate to determine your cash flow. Then from this statement, annual amounts can be estimated, taking into account seasonal variances. The budget statement should include an amount for savings. It is suggested that most families will need savings for long-term objectives to be a minimum of 15 percent of earned income.

Before embarking on an investment plan to accomplish your long-term goals, it is wise to establish building blocks, such as an emergency fund and an appropriate insurance program. The size of your emergency fund depends on factors such as your family income, number of income earners, and the stability of your employment. A minimum emergency fund is generally three to six months of family expenditures. I usually suggest the use of a mutual fund money market account for emergencies because it pays competitive interest rates without a surrender charge.

Insurance

Three rules, simple as they are, provide a basic framework for making decisions when purchasing insurance:

1. "Don't risk more than you can afford to lose." If the maximum potential exposure can be financially devastating, then you must purchase insurance.

2. "Consider the odds." The probability of loss affects the decision in a way different than most people think. A high probability means insurance is probably not an economical way of dealing with the risk, because an insurance company must charge the expected loss plus a profit. The best buys in insurance cover those losses that are the least likely to happen.

3. "Don't spend a lot for a little." This rule can be especially effective in determining the size of a deductible. Compare the cost of insurance with different deductibles and then evaluate if the lower deductible is worth the additional cost.

Long-Term Goals

To determine the amount of savings you need for long-term goals, projections should be made of what these goals will cost at the appropriate time in the future, and then reduced based on a reasonable projection of the interest earned on savings. The following is a simplified analysis of the savings needed to pay future college costs for a new-born baby, assuming an average annual cost of $6,000.

Item	Amount/Instructions
1. Number of years until college	18
2. Number of years in college	4
Amount desired:	
3. Cost in today's dollars	$24,000 (public college)
4. Future dollars 7% inflation	$81,120 (multiply #3 x 3.38)
Funds available:	
5. Current funds (if any)	$5,000
6. Future value at 9% earnings	$23,600 (multiply #5 x 4.72)
7. Additional funds required	$57,520 (subtract #6 - #4)
8. Annual savings needed at 9%	$1,265 (multiply #7 x .022)

Life insurance has emerged as the college funding vehicle of choice by many families because it provides tax deferral and death benefit protection. An ideal type of policy to meet this need is a "no-load no commission" universal life policy, because it has little to no surrender charge and generally provides an excellent rate of return given its safety. Another approach you should consider is the use of a 2503(c) trust. This irrevocable trust may pay taxes at a lower rate than a child under age 14 would normally have to use. This trust costs $250-$500 to develop.

Your financial plan should include an analysis similar to the one above for each long-term goal you have. Having such a plan does not guarantee success, but it should provide the type of foundation you desire for your family.

Choosing a financial planner

When considering an expert's assistance, it is important for you to know how he or she is compensated. Three methods of compensation exist today:

1. Commission only—requires the least financial commitment on your part, but provides the least detail in planning.

2. Fee based (fee plus commission)—generally provides a more detailed plan because a fee is paid for the plan.

3. Fee only—provides detailed plan and objective advice not influenced by commissions.

Once you understand a planner's method of compensation and the service he will provide, you should be able to choose the person that will best meet your needs.

Milton Hixson is a Certified Public Accountant and Certified Financial Planner associated with Financial Management Professions, Inc.

Austin Regional Clinic - Pediatric Division

The Austin Regional Clinic (A.R.C.) provides comprehensive, convenient health care to individuals and families throughout Central Texas. Austin Regional Clinic began as a multispecialty medical group in 1980 when Dr. Carol Faget (Pediatrics), Dr. Thomas P. Zavaleta (Pediatrics), and Dr. Norman Chenven (Family Practice) combined their practices. Since that time, A.R.C. has continued to grow, adding specialities in many areas of health care. There are now a total of 75 physicians associated with A.R.C., 16 of whom are pediatricians.

A.R.C. offers pediatric services in six locations to provide easy access for patients. With the remaining network of doctors, they are able to provide medical care for the whole family; the group has 12 subspecialities and offers a multitude of ancillary services.

All physicians are either Board Certified or Board eligible in their area of speciality. All locations have full lab and x-ray facilities, helping avoid travel time to obtain care. The physicians and staff are very dedicated and caring people who work hard at maintaining good communication with children and parents. A.R.C. sponsors parenting groups and offers courses open to the public concerning asthma, first aid, "latch-key" children, and other topics of interest.

As active supporters of the Brackenridge Foundation, the Child Abuse Prevention Project, and Caritas of Austin, A.R.C. is significantly involved in the health of the community at large.

A.R.C. provides treatment for illness, advocates prevention of disease, and encourages the maintenance of healthy lifestyles. The doctors and staff work with parent and child to keep the child healthy, both physically and psychologically, with an emphasis on keeping health-care costs affordable.

The pediatricians at A.R.C. encourage protection of children from illness and disease through immunization programs and well-child checkups. They emphasize the importance of good nutrition in developing a healthy lifestyle. "We are committed to providing responsive, personalized care, promoting healthy lifestyles, and maintaining the highest standards of professionalism."

A.R.C. physicians are participating providers of PruCare of Austin, Custom Care, Prudential Plus, and CHAMPUS. They also welcome patients who are private pay or who are covered by most types of major medical insurance.

Arbor Square Medical Center • 12871 Research Blvd. #105 • 250-9646
Barton Oaks Medical Center • 901 MoPac South #170 • 328-3888
Brodie Lane Medical Associates • 8204 Brodie Ln. #101 • 282-8967
Northwest Hills Medical Center • 6835 Austin Center Blvd. • 346-6611
Round Rock Family Medical Center • 2000 Mays #202 • 244-9024
South Austin Medical Associates • 3828 South First St. • 443-1311

24-Hour Telephone Number: 346-6611

Open 8-5, Monday — Friday. After-hours & weekend care are available at the Northwest office.

George F. Smith, M.D.

Dr. George F. Smith provides and arranges for all the health care needs of his patients ages six years and up. In private practice in Austin since 1980, Dr. Smith graduated from the University of Texas Medical Branch at Galveston and completed his residency at Central Texas Medical Foundation and Brackenridge Hospital. Dr. Smith is affiliated with South Austin Medical Center, where he is a member of the Board of Trustees and past chief of the medical staff.

As a family physician, Dr. Smith pays attention to all aspects of both physical and mental health. His knowledge of the family structure and family dynamics helps him determine all factors that affect health. He is able to treat personally 90 percent of all complaints arising in a family and has the ability to make appropriate referrals for unusual situations. A comfortable waiting room includes toys to keep children entertained.

Dr. Smith advises parents to choose day care carefully, making sure that it is adequate and appropriate to the child's needs. He also cautions parents to be alert to possible problems with drug abuse and recommends drug-abuse education and prevention programs.

The office is open late Wednesdays and every other Saturday to better accommodate the patient's needs. MasterCard and Visa are accepted, and the office will file hospitalization insurance forms.

George F. Smith, M.D. • 7201-B Manchaca Rd., • 443-3577
Open 9-5 Mon. - Fri., alternate Sat. mornings, 11-6 Wed.

Allen Sonstein, M.D.
Family Practice and Internal Medicine

Dr. Allen Sonstein provides comprehensive and continuous care for the entire family. A 1972 graduate of Jefferson Medical College, Dr. Sonstein is Board Certified in both Internal Medicine and Family Practice. He has been in private practice in Austin since 1978. His background enables him to deal with both simple and more complicated medical problems.

Dr. Sonstein is concerned about providing affordable medical care and has designed his practice so that he is accessible to his patients. Optimum health is always the goal of Dr. Sonstein and his staff. He believes that the more a patient knows about his health, the better able he will be to maintain a healthy life. Dr. Sonstein provides educational materials and places an emphasis on preventative medicine. The doctor talks with the patient and explains any issue of concern. Dr. Sonstein has a special interest in children ages 6 and up and in the problems of the handicapped. Bilingual staff is available. The office will file insurance for hospitalization.

Allen Sonstein, M.D. • 7201-B Manchaca Road • 443-3577
Hours vary; Call for appointment

Southwest Family Practice

William G. Franklin, M.D. delivers medical care in a family-oriented way. He believes in promoting good health through preventative care and by teaching good health habits to his patients. The clinic serves patients from newborn through geriatric and has staff privileges at Brackenridge Hospital, St. David's Hospital, and South Austin Medical Center.

A graduate of the University of Texas Medical Branch, Dr. Franklin has been in private practice in Austin since 1986. He strives to know all his patients well and offers personalized care to all members of the family. A strong focus on helping families develop a healthy lifestyle is reflected in the clinic's providing nutrition and exercise programs, as well as health care, for patients. A nutritionist on the staff works with psychologists, psychiatrists, therapists, and medical evaluations to provide a complete weight-loss program. The goal is to understand and change eating habits so that patients will be healthier and happier.

Dr. Franklin advises parents to create a positive, supportive, and loving environment for their children and to help them develop healthy diet and exercise habits that will serve them well through their lives.

The office accepts MasterCard and Visa and Travelers, Texas Health Plan, Partners, Pru-Plus, Custom Care, and Blue Cross/Blue Shield insurance.

Southwest Family Practice • 5316 Hwy 290 West #150 • 892-2990
Open 8-6 Monday - Friday, 9-12 Saturday

James R. Brown, M.D.

Dr. James R. Brown, a graduate of the University of Texas Medical School at Houston, established his practice in Austin in 1985 after serving a three-year residency at Brackenridge Hospital. His practice serves patients from infancy through geriatrics. A large part of the practice is devoted to preventative medicine and educating patients in how they can remain healthy.

Dr. Brown realizes that his patients are dependent upon him for their care, and he is always ready to listen and be available to them. Because he loves the practice of medicine and is very dedicated to his practice, patients find the office a warm and attentive place. Dr. Brown has staff privileges at Seton, Brackenridge, and South Austin Hospitals. The office accepts MasterCard and Visa. The staff is friendly and caring, and office hours can be flexible on request to accommodate patients' schedules.

James R. Brown, M.D.
706 West Martin Luther King, Suite 16 • 478-4137
Open Monday - Friday 8:30 am - 5 pm, Wed. 8:30 am - 12 noon

Andrew H. Weary, M.D.

Dr. Andrew Weary, a family practitioner, offers broad-based personally oriented health care for the whole family. The bilingual office (the doctor is fluent in Spanish) offers family planning, minor emergency care, and pediatrics along with other areas of health care. Because all members of the family are familiar to the doctor, he understands the dynamics going on between family members and treats each individual with his whole environment in mind.

A graduate of UT-Austin, Dr. Weary trained at Autonomous University of Guadalajara Medical School and the University of California at Irvine. He served his residency for Family Practice at Memorial Medical Center in Corpus Christi. He served as emergency hospital doctor in Southeast Texas and at Brooks Army Medical Center. He began practice in Austin in 1981. His office is open 8:30-4:30, Monday - Friday; Wednesdays, 8:30-noon; and Saturdays by appointment.

Andrew H. Weary, M.D.
4007 James Casey, Suite D-150 • 443-6035

Austin Regional Clinic - Family Practice

Arbor Square Medical Center • 12871 Research #105 • 250-9646
Barton Oaks Medical Center • 901 MoPac South #170 • 328-2888
Quail Creek Family Center • 9411 Parkfield Dr. #400-D • 836-3472

"And now may our hearts be open to all the children of the generations of man that the circle of love and peace may grow forevermore."
—Anonymous

Children's Hospital of Austin at Brackenridge

Children's Hospital of Austin at Brackenridge provides complete medical and surgical services for sick and injured children. It is the only children's hospital in Central Texas. Facilities include a Pediatric Intensive Care Center, a Day Surgery Center, and a wing for preteens and teens. The hospital also has the only Children's Emergency Center in Texas with regional service by STAR Flight emergency medical helicopter. The Specialty Care Center for children with prolonged diseases provides for evaluation and treatment, at one time in one location. Special emphasis is placed on meeting emotional needs, as well as physical ones, with highly specialized pediatric staff, the latest equipment, and facilities designed for the special needs of children. A supportive family environment promotes the healing process. Day beds are provided in each room for parents. The Parents Place serves as a valuable resource for education and support.

Children's Hospital of Austin at Brackenridge
601 East 15th Street • 480-1818

Seton Kids Care Club and Seton Sick Child Home Care

Seton offers unique care for sick children whose parents cannot stay at home to care for them. Seton Kids Care Club is a day care center for sick children who cannot stay at home. Children six months through 12 years are watched over by health professionals with special training in child care. A registered nurse is on duty at all times. A ratio of four children to one child care aide ensures that your child will have individual attention. Quiet games, books, toys, and videotapes are available to keep the child entertained.

Four separate rooms are maintained for kids with different illnesses: chicken pox, flu or stomach virus, colds and respiratory illnesses, and noncontagious ailments, such as broken legs and ear infections. The room for kids with chicken pox even has its own entrance and ventilation system. Every evening the rooms are thoroughly cleaned with hospital-strength disinfectant—including linens and toys. Child care aides are assigned to one specific room each day and do not travel to other rooms. Snacks and lunch are served in the individual rooms. Staff can see all the children through large interior windows. The windows also give the rooms an open feeling. Parents are welcome to visit any time. Please call before coming for a tour. When you call to reserve space for your child, a staff member will do an initial phone assessment, and when you arrive, a registered nurse will assess your child's symptoms. The nurse continues to check the children throughout the day. Check-in time is 6:30 am and check-out is 6 pm. Cost for the first child is $35/full day and $25/half day. Phone lines open at 6 am.

Seton also offers programs for care in the home. Families who are expecting or who have recently had a baby can receive health care at home through the Maternal Home Care program. Jaundiced newborns can take advantage of the Home Phototherapy program. The Neonatal Pediatric Home Care program provides highly sophisticated equipment and skilled care. The Sick Child Home Care helps working parents by providing a reliable adult sitter who will come to your home and look after your sick child.

Home health aides who have completed a certified nurse's aide course will arrive at your home and follow your directions in caring for your sick child. The aide will carefully monitor your child's condition and if necessary will notify an R.N. Personalized and comforting care makes you and your child feel secure and looked after. Rates are $7.50 per hour. Special full-time LVN care is available on request at additional cost.

Seton Kids Care Club • 476-5437 (476-KIDS) • 1003 West 6th
Seton Sick Child Home Care • 469-3260

Children's World Learning Centers

Children's World offers a broad range of activities for both parents and children. Children use individualized learning centers that allow them to choose their own activities in addition to group activities. Special events, such as story time, speakers, field trips, dance, gymnastics, computer training, and swimming are available. Summer camp is available for 5-12 year olds. A monthly parent newsletter keeps parents up to date on activities, and parent educational material provides information about each stage in a child's development.

Children's World believes that each child is a unique individual, and the staff is sensitive to each child's social, emotional, intellectual, and physical needs. They provide developmentally appropriate programs that focus on the process of learning and help children enjoy successful experiences. The staff encourages not only learning, but also the love of learning. The school maintains a lower child-to-teacher ratio than is required by the state, and ensures that teachers and staff are dedicated early childhood educators who are selected not only for their professional qualifications, but also for their warm, caring personalities. Fees may be paid weekly, monthly, or bi-monthly. Children between the ages of 6 weeks and 12 years are accepted, and before- and after-school care is available.

Children's World Learning Centers
7130 Chimney Corners • 346-6160 • 12001 Oak Knoll Dr. • 250-1669
1808 Cedar Bend Dr. • 832-9137 • 6434 South Congress • 443-7765
Open 6:30 am - 6:30 pm, Monday - Friday

Children's Discovery Center

Dianne Arnett has been in the child care business for the past 15 years and established her school in 1979 to provide individual attention to each child, enhance each child's self-confidence and self-esteem, and provide positive reinforcement as a child grows. The school creates a family environment in a charming old home with a low student-to-staff ratio where each child can learn independence and new skills. Guest speakers and programs, as well as field trips, dance, gymnastics, music, and swimming, enhance the learning programs.

The school provides two healthy snacks a day and maintains a consistent schedule that is so important to children. Programs are available to help with parenting, and parents are always welcome at the school. In this purposely small school, every child from ages 18 months to 6 years is special.

Children's Discovery Center
4112 Duval Street • 458-1891 • Open 7:30 am to 6 pm

Creative World Learning Centers

Doug and Denise Kniffin founded the Creative World Learning Centers to provide quality education and child care, beginning with 12-month olds and extending through after-school care. Doug's background as a psychologist and Denise's training in Early Childhood Education create an environment where children enjoy the process of learning. Their commitment to developmentally appropriate education has been demonstrated in the various programs they have developed—ranging from toddler/pre-school care to a strong academically based private school (kindergarten through third).

Creative World provides a nurturing environment that encourages children to take an active role in their learning. The professionally trained staff, large classrooms, specially designed play area, and structured educational curriculum provide the quality care your child deserves. Carefully planned programs will allow your child to create and discover, develop friendships, and benefit from positive guidance. Creative World maintains a lower student/teacher ratio than is required by the state, and has on-going training and support for the staff in the areas of program development, lesson planning, and curriculum. Programs have been developed for Toddlers (1-2 years), Pre-School (3 years), and Pre-Kindergarten (4 years), with a separate facility for private kindergarten through third grade and before- and after-school care (K-5).

Creative World Learning Centers
2020 Denton Drive at Metric Boulevard • 837-8822 • Open 6:30-6:30

Anderson Creative Learning Centers , Inc.
Six locations • Infants through 1st grade & after-school care
A school where learning to learn is fun.
837-2821

Hyde Park Baptist Child Development Center
3901 Speedway • 465-8383
Nurturing environment for the emotional, cognitive, social, spiritual & physical growth of infants-5 yrs.; elementary after-school & summers. NAEYC Accredited

Kids Playhouse Inc.
1818 W. Ben White Blvd. • 443-9246 • 8490 Burnet Rd. • 452-7880
State licensed drop-in child care • Security system
Ages 18 mo—12 years • Day & Night • Hourly rates

Clothing/Furniture

Bright Beginnings

Bright Beginnings offers 100 percent cotton clothing in fun, whimsical designs that are both practical and comfortable for sizes newborn to 8-10. Owner Sally Whitehouse opened the store after being unable to find high-quality, well-priced, good-looking clothing for her own children. She carefully chooses all of the items available in the shop, paying close attention to avoid tight bands, scratchy lace, and movement-restricting styles. Many of the clothes in her store are hand-sewn, painted, dyed, and detailed with comfort, style, price, and appearance in mind. The child's point of view is a top priority—kids like the look and feel of 100 percent cotton. A specially designed play area for children includes TV, VCR, and toys, and a puppet-show stage keep the kids happy while parents shop. Visa and MasterCard are accepted, and layaway and gift certificates are available.

Bright Beginnings • 1006 W. 38th St. • 454-5437
Open: Monday - Friday, 9-6; Saturday, 10-6

Expecting The Best

Expecting The Best is a store dedicated to the needs of prospective mothers and infants. Charles Sikes, owner, has been in the business for 32 years and knows how to find just the right items for his customers. Maternity wear, nursing needs, infant's clothing, baby gift items, and accessories for preemies to 24 months make up the unusual merchandise mix. Service is of primary importance.

The focus of the shop is on providing tasteful and moderately priced maternity wear. A large selection lets you tailor your wardrobe to your particular lifestyle. Whether you need clothing for work, sportswear, or evening finery, you'll find it at Expecting The Best. The shop features coordinated crib bedding, a shower registry service, and a monthly newsletter for customers. Among the many unique pieces is a selection of strollers, including the jogging stroller. Layaway and gift wrapping are available. The store is one block from Seton Hospital.

Expecting The Best • 1000 W. 39th at Lamar • 452-2422 or 452-2438
Open Monday - Saturday, 9:30-6

The Hills—A Healthcare Fitness Center

A Healthcare Fitness Center

The Hills is a fitness center located on approximately ten acres of beautiful Austin hill country. Strengthening equipment, exercise classes, swimming, jogging trails, racquetball and squash courts, basketball court, sauna, steamroom, and whirlpool facilities are just some of the options available at The Hills. There is also a cafe specializing in low-fat, low-sodium, high-fiber foods. Babysitting is available while Mom gets back in shape.

As a community resource, The Hills is a leader in offering professionally designed programs to meet individual or group needs. The focus of the program is "Wellness," the optimum balance of physical, mental, and emotional health. Members benefit in many ways, including improved cardiovascular conditioning, relief from stress, better resistance to illness, increased energy and endurance, and greater enthusiasm for life.

The Hills also offers massage therapy and counseling on nutrition and smoking cessation, as well as individual fitness programs. Whatever your needs in terms of getting fit or staying fit, The Hills is prepared to meet them. In Austin since 1980, The Hills has served people of all ages, professions, and fitness levels from beginner to the serious athlete. Staff members have backgrounds in exercise physiology, physical education, recreation, and more. In addition, they receive specialized training at The Hills.

The Hills will provide an individual health evaluation, including cholesterol test, cardiac endurance test, and flexibility and strength tests, so that you will know exactly what you need to get fit. In addition, The Hills offers creative movement, gymnastics, and swimming classes for children, plus special classes for members presented by outside professionals to answer specific member questions. From time to time, special vacation packages are also offered.

The Hills' professional fitness staff is available to assist members in any exercise activity, class, or program. Membership is on a monthly basis. Corporate and individual rates are available, and Visa, MasterCard, and American Express are accepted. The Hills is open Monday through Friday from 6 am until 9 pm, Saturdays from 8 am until 6 pm, and Sundays from 12 noon until 6 pm.

The Hills
4615 Bee Caves Road • 327-4881

Nutri Link

Dr. William G. Franklin has established a weight-loss and maintenance program based on his experience as a family physician. The Nutri Link system is a two-phased program that involves a protein-sparing modified fast (a liquid diet) and an intensive behavior-modification program designed to treat the underlying causes of overeating and prevent relapses of bad eating habits.

For those who don't want to maintain a completely liquid diet, a modified version has been created. The program works well because weight loss is very rapid. The program is also easy to follow since there are no choices of menu, the patient is never hungry, and he or she has plenty of energy.

The overall goal of the program is to make permanent changes in the patient's lifestyle so that an optimum weight can be easily maintained. Psychiatrists, psychologists, and therapists conduct group sessions to find the underlying causes of overeating, prevent relapse, and learn new ways of behavior. The group sessions may be attended for six months free of charge once you have attained your weight goals. As part of the program, patients receive a physical exam and comprehensive lab testing. Medical monitoring is conducted every other week, and an exercise program is provided. On-staff nutritionists design a personalized diet for each patient's maintenance program.

Nutri Link • 5316 Hwy 290 West • 892-2990
Open 8-6 Monday - Friday, 9-12 Saturday

Seton Good Health School • 465-3131
Three locations in Austin
Tips and classes on parenting, maternity care,
fitness, nutrition, and stress

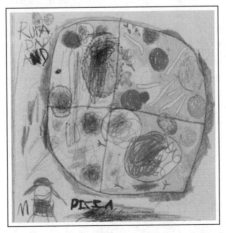

by Ruth Perzynska, age 5, The Montessori Center

Financial Management Professionals, Inc.

Financial Management Professionals, Inc. is a comprehensive financial planning firm registered as an Investment Adviser with the Securities and Exchange Commission. The firm provides broad-based financial planning services for its clients with an emphasis on investment diversification. Their service helps you set your financial goals, assess your current financial situation, consider the ramifications of various planning alternatives, choose an investment strategy which will help you accomplish your goals, and adjust your planning methods in accordance with the changing economic environment. The company considers virtually all investment devices in providing investment advice to clients. There is no minimum fee, and the fee structure is based on the complexity of the client's financial situation. The firm does not charge commissions in addition to established fees.

Incorporated in 1987, Milton Hixson and Kenneth Jones are planners and advisers. Milton Hixson, C.P.A., C.F.P., was previously employed by Arthur Andersen & Co., Magnolia Life Insurance Company, and Hixson Turner & Co. Ken Jones, C.P.A., was employed by Heard McElroy and Vestal and by Bounds Chatelain and Co. before joining Financial Management Professionals, Inc.

The firm offers comprehensive financial planning, beginning with a review of the client's total financial situation and concluding with the preparation of a comprehensive individualized written financial plan. The recommendations include specific methods to save income taxes, to improve cash flow, and to make investments that will help the client attain his or her financial goals. At all times, careful attention is paid to the individual client's level of risk tolerance.

An option provided by the firm is an investment monitoring service. This service provides monitoring and asset allocation recommendations with regard to the client's risk tolerance and overall portfolio objectives. The adviser will also assist the client in gathering the data, establishing objectives, and identifying the constraints that affect the selection of a particular type of pension plan. The client may also engage the adviser on an hourly basis to undertake an examination of a specific area of an individual's financial situation.

Financial Management Professionals presents informative seminars and workshops on general topics, such as income tax saving strategies, budgeting, debt management, investment planning, etc. These sessions help participants understand general principles regarding the subjects.

The office is open from 9 am until 6 pm. Call for an appointment.

Financial Management Professionals, Inc.
1717 West 6th St., Suite 120 • 328-7283

Lance Hurley, C.F.P.

Lance graduated from the University of Texas and did graduate work at Arizona State University. Lance is a Chartered Life Underwriter, a Chartered Financial Consultant, a Certified Financial Planner and is admitted to the registry of Financial Planning Practitioners. He is the only financial planner in Central Texas to have all four of these designations. As a Registered Investment Adviser, Lance offers complete financial planning analysis and implementation. He is a Registered Principal with LNC Equity Sales, Inc. and a Registered Broker Dealer Member of NASD and SIPC.

Lance offers a full range of investment products, including discount brokerage. He also advises on life, disability, medical, and nursing home insurance. Working closely with clients, their attorneys, and C.P.A.s, Hurley utilizes his twenty years' experience in developing a sound plan commensurate with the client's goals and objectives. He believes financial planning should be an ongoing process and works with people to make that process comfortable and pleasant.

Lance Hurley, C.F.P.
One Northpoint Center, Suite 115 • 328-3514
Hours by appointment Monday—Friday, 8-5

Delta Co Financial Services

Phyllis Dell is a Certified Financial Planner with a background in real estate, securities, and insurance. She opened Delta Co in 1986 to provide help with complete financial planning, real estate, and mortgages. She evaluates clients' financial needs to secure future goals and recommends courses of action. A special program is available to help people select the mortgage type best suited to their needs. She also offers several mortgage acceleration plans. She is interested in helping young families through the potential problems they face in securing their financial futures. The office accepts Visa and MasterCard. Call for an appointment Monday-Friday, 8-5.

Delta Co Financial Services
5828 Balcones, Suite 104 • 454-7633

Chris John, Chartered Financial Consultant

Money 101, A Prerequisite to Adult Money Management

Chris John teaches a class entitled Money 101, a hands-on instructional course in financial planning, in which participants learn how to develop and monitor their own financial plan. The course is easy to understand and follow, whether or not you have ever had any money-management training. The highly participative workshop uses examples and case studies (for example, college funding alternatives). You will not be asked to reveal personal financial information. Chris John is a Chartered Financial Consultant and has been admitted to the prestigious Registry of Financial Planning Practitioners.

Resource Consulting Group, Inc.
500 West 6th Street, Suite 301 • 478-8779

by Yogi Gouda, age 6, Isley School

CHAPTER II

Trials and Tribulations of Toddlerhood

(1-3 years)

by Joo Young Shin, Grade 2, Matthews Elementary School

The Toddler

by Gail Allen and Karen Haslund, M.D.

A toddler is curious, affectionate, demanding, enthusiastic, stubborn as a mule, and wondrous. A toddler's "job" is to develop his independence as he sensorially experiences the world for the first time. The parents' job, on the other hand, is not nearly as defined. As parents we know some key words like "guidance" and "safety," "setting limits," and how could I forget about "quality time?" The questions are not as much about "What should I do?" as they are about "How do I do it?" Toddler time for parents can be both delightful and exhausting.

The one- to three-year-old child still believes that he is the only person on the planet who has needs and desires—and that they must be met now! He wants to be center stage—not only a one-man show—he innocently believes he's the only show in town. Our toddler is unable to delay gratification, so his schedule is the only schedule that matters. Sometimes he remembers the rules, and sometimes he will care only about his needs being met immediately. A perfect example is a hungry toddler. Have you ever seen a hungry, screaming toddler respond to a parent's "Honey, I'm fixing dinner. It will be ready in a few minutes," with "Sure, mom, I'll sit quietly over here and relax."?

Here are a few suggestions on how to set up your home environment to support your toddler's goals of developing independence and self-esteem. You will notice the concentration on supporting self-help skills.

1. Have stools to reach sinks in both bathrooms and kitchens for handwashing and other clean-up tasks. Purchase child-size mops, brooms, and dustpans. This is the age when little ones are thrilled to "help" Mommy or Daddy. They will feel so proud of their contribution to family life. Our caution to parents is to arrange these "helpful times" when you are rested and in good humor. If you are in a hurry or preoccupied, then wait for another opportunity.

2. In the kitchen, have a low cabinet where toddlers can find their cup, dish, eating utensils, napkin, and sponge. Place a small plastic pitcher with a top and a controlled spout on the bottom shelf of the refrigerator so the toddler can pour his own juice. You'll hear and see the success simultaneously. "Mommy, I did it!" will erupt from that beaming face.

3. Select clothes that are easy to put on: low-top tennis shoes with velcro instead of high tops with laces • elastic-waist pants • large buttons for small fingers • front openings • sunsuits with double-knot ties that easily slip off shoulders • mittens on strings, strung through coat arms • coats with hoods attached

4. For hungry, cranky toddlers, have small prepared snacks ready in the fridge. Also, bring some snacks with you in the car for after a long day at day care. Sometimes, cut-up fruit or peanut butter crackers are all you'll need to prevent a full-fledged tantrum in a car seat at the most vulnerable time of the day for both of you.

Here are a few behaviors that you may experience with your toddler during the next year or two:

1. "NO!" is a powerful word that frequently expresses autonomy, fueled by the toddler's drive toward independence. "No" frequently means "I am me!" "Wait, don't rush me," "I will choose," "I can do it," as well as "I don't want to." You should only offer choices to toddlers when either "yes" or "no" are accept-

able answers. You can see how some of the following choices could create a power struggle: "Sweetheart, are you ready for a nap?" "Do you want to leave the playground now?" These questions are appropriate if "no" would be an acceptable response. If not, try these in a kind and firm voice: "It is nap time." "I know you want to stay, and it is time to leave."

2. Biting, hitting, hair pulling, grabbing. You may often experience short periods of these aggressive behaviors as your child moves through toddlerhood. Toddlers are only just beginning to develop social skills. Grabbing seems to be one of their main communication styles. It is important to remember that the lack of developed language skills is a contributing factor to a toddler's low frustration tolerance. As a child's vocabulary increases, so does his ability to express his feelings in words. As he begins to experience words as effective communication tools, these behaviors will disappear.

In the meantime, here are a few suggestions to help you cope:

1. Prevention. Know your child's frustration signals. Sometimes a quick distraction may be all that is needed.

2. Set the limit for appropriate behavior in a firm tone, and when appropriate, use substitution: "Biting people is absolutely not O.K. Here—bite this, hit this, pull this," "People are not for hitting," "I know you're angry and I will not be hit," and then place the child firmly away from your body. (This is a powerful message because you have used both verbal and non-verbal communication.) Hitting or biting back only escalates the behavior and gives the child a very mixed message. Our job as parents is to role model problem-solving techniques and communication skills.

3. The most effective technique in dealing with wailing, whining, and tantrums is to ignore them. A tantrum is a performance for an audience. If the audience leaves, the show will wind down. Other techniques are: Physically remove the child with kindness from any danger and place him or her in a boring place (no audience) with words such as, "I know you're mad. You can be mad here." Another alternative, just in case the performer follows you, is to quietly remove yourself to a spot out of sight but within earshot. The non-verbal message is, "I will not be around this screaming." A word about "time-out." It is simply a few moments for a child to experience the consequences of his actions. It should be brief—one minute for each year of the child's age. A timer can keep it neutral.

Finally, we would like to stress the importance of daily routines and rituals that toddlers can depend on and look forward to—from early morning routines to loving tender bedtimes. These daily occurrences will create an atmosphere of safety and security—an atmosphere that can only foster independence and a sense of well-being.

Life with a toddler was once described to us as a "dance." Sometimes the dance has rhythms and grace and partnership. Sometimes the dance is more fun than you've had in a very long time. At other times, it feels like a slam dance full of resistance with both partners leading in opposite directions, with all toes sore from the rough handling. Guaranteed, your toddler will skip back and forth between dependence and independence frequently. So our best advice is: "Keep your dancing shoes on and the dance will be worth every step."

Gail Allen is a child and family communications consultant, workshop leader and Montessori educator. Karen Haslund, M.D., is a pediatrician.

Meeting Nutritional Needs

by Teresa Amos, R.D./L.D.

Nutrition is our ammunition against disease. It protects health, growth, and well-being throughout life. "Fueling" needs change in response to age, life-cycle stage, activity level, and condition. Eating habits develop early in life in response to physiological capability, developmental factors, and psycho-social dynamics. The general nutrition principles of variety, moderation, and balance are important to ensure a high quality of life at all ages.

In-utero nutrient needs are met passively via the placental connection with the mother. Demands are high, as this is the fastest growth period we experience in our lives. Growth in infancy (the first year of life) only slightly decelerates. Food choices are largely based on physiological capabilities. Our capability to digest and absorb food is limited during this time. Our food must initially be liquid and easy to digest like breastmilk or special infant formula. We cannot chew or otherwise manipulate many textures in our mouth until the second half of the first year. Our kidneys cannot handle excessive loads of sodium or protein by-products during that first year. Large volumes cannot be tolerated as stomach capacity is limited.

By one year of age, the onset of toddlerhood, many of these physiological limitations have been resolved. Digestive juices are now present at levels that make eating a variety of solid foods and properly digesting them possible. Kidney function approaches that of an adult so that whole milk, a natural sodium source, and other high-protein foods can be introduced. Tooth development that began at five to seven months of age will soon be complete at 18 months of age. Texture should be matched to the individual toddler's stage of dentition. If your toddler has less than six teeth, very soft and mashed foods would still be best. If your toddler has between six and twelve teeth, soft finger foods and lumpy junior/table foods could safely be served. If your toddler has more than 12 teeth, most soft table foods will be tolerated. Toddlers don't have mature chewing capabilities until about two and one-half years of age. Never leave them to eat a meal or snack alone to avoid a choking accident.

Growth begins to slow during toddlerhood. A decrease in appetite and interest in food ensues. Since the toddler is still small and does not have much room in his stomach, small, frequent feedings continue to be necessary. Offer three meals and two or three snacks each day. Milk, water, and juice should be given in adequate but not excessive amounts so that fullness does not interfere with solid food intake. An adequate amount of fluid is one to one and one-half quarts each day. Since appetite may be compromised, foods offered for meal and snacktime should be of high nutrient density. Avoid foods that provide a high measure of calories from sugar or fat. Healthy snack choices include yogurt, fruit, or cheese and crackers.

Sweets or high-fat snack foods should only be served in very small amounts. Don't use them as bribes or withhold them as punishment. The child bribed to eat wholesome foods with a promise of a sweet reward soon learns that the sweet reward has more value. Desserts can be served on the plate with the meal to give them a more neutral role in the development of eating habits.

Avoid battles at the dinner table. Toddler response to being pressured to eat is to dig in their heels to maintain as much of their treasured new-found independence as possible. Ellyn Satter, MSW/RD, points out in her work that to avoid food fights, take note of the natural division of responsibility. It is the responsibility of the parent to select and buy food, make and present meals, regulate the time of meals and snacks, provide food in age-appropriate format, help the child attend to the task of eating, and maintain standards of behavior. The child determines how much he eats or whether he eats.

The planned wholesome snack is the parent's secret weapon. If the toddler eats poorly at a meal, signal clearly when the meal is over and assure him that more food will be available at the next scheduled meal or snack. Avoid being a short-order cook or allowing your child to panhandle between meals and snacks.

Often the toddler's self-feeding skills lag behind the emergence of his or her independent behavior. Finger foods can be an important nutritional source for these toddlers. Finger foods can be any food about the size and texture of a french fry. Steamed carrot coins, green beans, cheese strips, chicken cubes, bagel/muffin/tortilla pieces, and dry cereal are only a few representatives from the four food groups. One important parent survival skill is to know your child's nutritional needs. Toddlers generally need between 1,000-1,300 calories a day. Serving sizes are one-fourth to one-half the size of an adult serving.

DAILY FOOD GROUP CHART	Serving size
Milk group (4 servings)	
whole milk, yogurt, milk-based soup	1/2 cup
cheese	1/2 ounce
cottage cheese	2-4 T
pudding, ice cream, ice milk	2-4 T
Meat/Meat alternatives group (2-3 servings)	
beef, chicken, turkey, fish	2 T/1 ounce
egg	1
peanut butter (2 yrs and over)	1 T
beans/legumes	1/4-1/3 cup
Fruit/Vegetable group (4 servings)	
vitamin C source—citrus fruit, melon, tomato, broccoli, peppers, cabbage, cauliflower, potato	1/3-1/2 cup
vitamin A source—deep green, yellow, orange fruits or	3-4 times a week
vegetables	1/4-1/2 cup
Bread and Cereal group (4 servings)	
bread, tortilla, bagel, muffin	1/2
rice or pasta	1/4-1/3 cup
cereal	1/2-3/4 ounce
Fat group	3 servings

Toddler intake is often erratic. The best way to look at your child's intake is to keep a food diary for seven days. List the type and amount of food, then average the number of servings from each food group consumed over that week. Compare this average to the Daily Food Group Chart. This will give you a more accurate picture than just looking at intake on a day-to-day basis. Discuss your child's growth chart with his/her doctor. The growth chart is the best gauge of nutritional success, and each child has his own individual growth pattern.

Teresa Amos, R.D./L.D., is a private nutrition consultant and pediatric specialist.

Your Child's First Dental Visit

by Albert M. Tate, Jr., D.D.S., M.S.D.

"When should I take my child to the dentist for the first visit?" This often-asked question receives different answers, and confusion usually follows. A common-sense approach to attain a head start on preventive dentistry and a future of reduced dental problems has been developed.

An introductory visit between nine and 12 months of age is ideal; several teeth have already erupted, and the parents should have already begun to brush the teeth and gums. The first visit is primarily an educational visit to make sure that proper oral hygiene, diet control, and other preventive measures are understood and practiced. A quick, thorough look at the teeth, gums, and soft tissues of the mouth is important. Observation of any problems and treatment indications can be discussed and implemented as needed.

Dental caries (cavities) may be seen very early, and in young children are most often caused by nursing-bottle syndrome. This is the name given to decay caused by frequent nursing or feeding from a bottle, which causes decay to start on the newly erupted teeth. Milk or juice frequently bathing teeth that aren't free of dental plaque can cause primary teeth to decay rapidly. Frequent brushing will minimize the effects of nursing-bottle syndrome; however, it may not eliminate the cavity-causing effects entirely.

An early dental visit can prevent problems from starting, or suggestions can be made to correct existing problems. Cavities can cause pain, infection, poor eating habits, and early loss of teeth. Baby teeth in the back of the mouth are usually not lost until age twelve; early loss can lead to space loss, which, in turn, usually causes orthodontic problems.

Prevention is the main emphasis in the first dental visit. Flouride should be discussed to determine proper flouridated water intake and possible indications for home flouride applications. Good brushing techniques, diet control, and other preventive measures can be discussed to make sure there is a good understanding by the parents of what can be done to prevent decay.

Some suggestions to help make dental visits fun for the child include reading a short book on dental visits. This will help your child prepare for the different environment that will be seen—the dental chair, the bright light, a dental mirror. Use encouraging words such as "fun," "count your teeth," "pretty smile," "learn about tooth care," "easy chair," and remember to avoid words such as "pain," "hurt," "pull," "shot," or "fear." Also try not to show any of your own apprehension by being too overprotective. The visits can be relaxed and fun if approached properly.

The first regular preventive dental visit should occur around age three. If earlier observation visits have occurred, then the introduction to the office is easier. If it is a first visit, then just seeing the "lay of the land" helps ease the child into the new environment. The preventive visit serves multiple purposes. The dentist will make a comprehensive diagnosis of the oral cavity, help the child and parent understand home care, and perform actual dental treatment (cleaning and flouride treatment, for example). It is important for the parent to understand that all of these areas may not be comfortably completed in one visit if there is too much apprehension on the child's part. The dentist and the staff will make a judgment on what is best for the child, then recommend the steps be accomplished in one or two visits.

There are many different ways children are introduced to dental evaluations, but basically a "Tell, Show, and Do" format works best. You can't rush children, so time is taken to help them become comfortable with the dentist and the environment before examination or prophylaxis is attempted.

The examination includes the evaluation of the soft tissues of the mouth to determine normal development and health of structures surrounding the teeth. The function of the jaws, occlusion (bite) of the teeth and normal swallowing, speech, and chewing are observed. The teeth are evaluated for normal size, spacing, development, number, and abnormalities, as well as for dental caries (decay).

Dental Radiographs (x-rays) may be indicated at the first preventive visit. The x-rays show development of permanent teeth, missing teeth, extra teeth, and abnormalities such as cysts, as well as the possible presence of decay. The planned and selective conservative use of dental x-rays is an important, integral part of a proper comprehensive evaluation of oral health.

The preventive part of the dental visit consists of cleaning the teeth with a special prophylaxis paste that removes stains and plaque from the teeth. The paste usually has flouride added to it to help in the hardening of the tooth enamel. After a thorough cleaning, the application of flouride is accomplished by applying a gel of flouride to the teeth. The flouride hardens the enamel, thereby making the teeth more resistant to decay. Flouride applications work only on erupted teeth and enhance the effectiveness of flouride in drinking water. The combined effects of flouride treatments every six months and flouride in the proper amount in drinking water can significantly reduce dental decay and the cost of dental care.

A discussion of proper eating habits and ideas about how to avoid dietary habits that increase the incidence of decay is a part of the first visit. Suggestions of how, when, and what to use at home to maintain optimum oral hygiene can increase the effectiveness of preventive care.

A question-and-answer wrap-up of the first visit is always interesting and can complete the visit by providing you with all you need to know about caring for your child's teeth. Getting started on the right foot and learning the basics of good dental health can lead to a lifetime of healthy mouths and smiles.

Albert Tate is a pediatric dentist who has been in practice in Austin since 1969.

by Rebekah Koeninger, age 4, Lake Austin Montessori

Ear, Nose and Throat Problems:
What Are the Facts?

by Stephen F. Conley, M.D., F.A.A.P.

At first glance, you must wonder what an otolaryngologist is and when would your child ever need to see one. First of all, an otolaryngologist is a physician-surgeon trained to diagnose, treat, and operate on disorders of the head and neck region, in all ages. A pediatric otolaryngologist has additional interest and training in treating the problems encountered in the ears, nose, and throat in infants, children, and adolescents. He or she might be consulted by your primary care doctor for care of your children at various times in their development.

The most common problem that an otolaryngologist confronts is the management of recurrent ear infections and evaluation of possible hearing loss. In our society with both parents frequently working, many infants and small children attend day-care centers where they catch frequent colds (upper respiratory infections). Blockage of the eustachian tube (the connection between the ear and throat) due to conditions such as frequent colds, enlarged adenoids, nasal drainage, or allergy can cause fluid to accumulate behind the ear drum. This generally results in two problems: 1. recurrent ear infections, and 2. hearing loss due to the fluid reducing sound transmission through the middle ear. If the fluid remains behind the ear drum for too long, permanent hearing loss could occur. The two most common periods of childhood for this problem are between birth and three years and between five and seven years.

Your primary care doctor will try to clear the infections and/or fluid with antibiotics. If this fails, then a tiny silicone tube can be placed in the ear drum to bypass the blocked eustachian tube, allowing air to pass freely into the middle ear cavity and the fluid to drain. The tube stays in position for about six to nine months and then is gradually pushed out by normal growth of the skin that covers the ear drum. The ear drum usually heals without any problems. Parents should expect tubes to be considered by their doctor after their child has had four or five ear infections in twelve months or if the ear fluid does not clear on antibiotics after two to three months. Decreased hearing in a child can be diagnosed by a hearing test in the otolaryngologist's office and is frequently helpful in determining the need for tube placement. Ventilation tubes essentially eliminate retention of fluid behind the ear drum and can prevent most recurrent ear infections, but water cannot be allowed to get into the ear canal because the ventilation tube will also allow water to enter the middle ear cavity and thus cause an ear infection.

Another frequent problem seen by an otolaryngologist is the complaint of snoring or chronic mouth breathing. Aside from being a nuisance, especially to the sibling who sleeps in the same room, snoring can have a far-reaching impact on the child. Chronic nasal obstruction frequently occurs in the three to seven year old and is most commonly due to enlarged adenoids or allergy. The adenoid is like the tonsil, but is located in the back of the nose up behind the roof of the mouth (palate). When the nose is obstructed, the child takes the easy route of breathing through the mouth all the time. This can cause changes in dental structures and facial features that may require orthodontics and/or surgery to correct. The otolaryngologist can help differentiate the causes of nasal obstruction and, if the adenoid pad is the offender, remove the adenoid and thus relieve the obstruction. If the child can then be retaught to nasal breathing, the changes in dental structures and facial features can be prevented.

The most frequent cause of loud snoring in children is due to enlargement of the adenoids and tonsils. Most snoring is intermittent in children and is harmless, but excessively loud and/or constant snoring may indicate a degree of true upper airway obstruction that can cause sleep disturbance, or rarely, more severe problems such as heart failure. An otolaryngologist can diagnose this problem through a complete history and physical examination. Additional tests may be helpful, such as x-rays, sleep studies, or a tape recording of the child sleeping. If airway obstruction is diagnosed, then removal of the tonsils and adenoids frequently cures the problem.

An otolaryngologist is also trained to diagnose and treat the occasional "lumps and bumps" that may appear in a child's neck and are usually something as simple as an enlarged node. These may also, however, be due to a congenital tissue mass left behind from when the baby was developing, or, rarely, a possible tumor. Most people do not think of a child as needing plastic surgery, but a child with protruding ears frequently benefits from having them "pinned back" before the child starts school and is subject to classmate teasing. Both minor and major problems of your child's head and neck region, therefore, are the concern of pediatric otolaryngologists, and they are available to your primary care doctor to help give your growing child the very best of care.

Stephen F. Conley, M.D., F.A.A.P., is Board Certified by the American Board of Otolaryngology and the American Board of Pediatrics. He is Assistant Clinical Professor at the University of Texas Health Science Center in San Antonio.

by Cale Sikes, age 4, Hyde Park Baptist Child Development Center

When Your Child Needs Plastic Surgery

by Robert A. Ersek, M.D., F.A.C.S.

Plastic surgery (or reconstructive surgery) is the medical specialty that deals with both form and function of the parts of the body. Not only is the plastic surgeon trained to repair non-functioning parts, but also to repair them so that their appearance is as pleasing as possible. The effect of disfiguration on a child's self-image and the response of others to the child must not be overlooked. Parents are most apt to consult a plastic surgeon when children are born with a congenital defect or sustain injury to their face or hands.

Parents should be aware that whenever a child's face or hands are injured, a plastic surgeon should be consulted immediately. All emergency rooms and hospitals have a board-certified plastic surgeon on call twenty-four hours a day. Whenever a child's face or hands are injured, parents should specifically request that a plastic surgeon be consulted by the emergency room physician. Even the most seemingly trivial injuries can result in devastating consequences if not treated appropriately.

CONGENITAL DEFECTS:

Congenital defects such as cleft lip, cleft palate, extra digits, or missing parts often require plastic surgery in infancy. Usually these defects are noted by the delivering obstetrician or pediatrician, but occasionally they are noted first by the parents. If any defect is suspected, the pediatrician should be consulted first, and then a plastic surgeon should be called in for consultation. Every city has a list of plastic surgeons in the telephone book yellow pages. All board-certified plastic surgeons have some training and knowledge of congenital defects. The more complex the problem, however, the more experience and skill the surgeon needs to correct it. Also, very complex problems require complex facilities for full treatment. Your surgeon can and should explain your particular situation and the steps needed to correct the problem.

Hemangioma or lymphangioma are conditions that are sometimes present at birth and that require treatment by a plastic surgeon. They are dilations of blood vessels or lymph vessels that cause soft bumps under the skin that range from the size of a pea to the size of a football. Sometimes they destroy surrounding structures as they grow and require prompt treatment. The plastic surgeon can remove the bumps and prevent further damage to surrounding tissue while at the same time minimizing scar tissue.

Cleft lip is a defect caused by failure of some of the parts of the lip to fuse when they are forming in the uterus. The condition is immediately recognizable at birth. Not only does the condition mar the appearance of the child, but it can also cause difficulty in speech. Cleft lip is usually repaired within the first few months of life, and if taken care of quickly causes little problem later in life.

Cleft palate is a defect in the hard or soft palate inside the mouth. Cleft palate may cause difficulty in pronunciation and eating, in addition to being visually unattractive. The severity of the cleft determines the difficulty the child may experience. Cleft palates are usually repaired when the child is between the ages of three and five years.

Extra digits, missing digits, or hand deformities are congenital defects that may affect the child's ability to function throughout life. Depending on the severity of the problem, extensive reconstructive surgery may be required.

ACCIDENTS AND TRAUMA:

Whenever a child is injured and requires emergency treatment, parents are naturally frightened and concerned. As alarming as it may be, however, it is not unusual for parents to have to visit the emergency room at some time when they have growing children. Parents should be aware that emergency rooms all have plastic surgeons on call, day and night, in the event that they are needed. If your child sustains a hand or face injury, you should ask that a plastic surgeon look at the injury—even if the emergency room attendant does not suggest it.

Injuries to the face can be repaired, but the manner in which they are repaired determines how your child will look to himself and to others for the rest of his life. Immediate care by a plastic surgeon can often avoid unsightly scarring and nerve damage and ensure that the wound will heal in the most aesthetic manner. Although children may be pleased at the badge of honor that stitches confer at the time, later in life they will appreciate the extra effort you (and the plastic surgeon) expend to make scars as invisible as possible.

Hands are delicate and well-designed tools that we use every day for both simple and complex tasks. The functioning of the hand is inextricably bound to the form that hand takes. It is important, therefore, that a plastic surgeon be involved in any reconstruction or treatment of hand injuries. Thousands of tiny muscles, blood vessels, nerves, and tendons make the hand operate as an efficient tool. When these connections are disturbed, it takes a specialist to reconnect and make the hand functional again.

Plastic surgery deals with the restoration of form and function, always aiming at achieving the optimum function and the most attractive form. While perfection eludes us, great improvements in reconstruction make it possible to virtually rebuild portions of the body that have been damaged or are missing.

Robert A. Ersek, M.D., is a board-certified Plastic and Reconstructive Surgeon who has been in practice in Austin since 1975.

by T.R. Zambraro, age 6, Kirby Hall School

Toys and Toddlers: Play It Safe

by Elise H. Ragland

Have you noticed how your toddler will bang on a toy or throw it and look or reach inside to see how it works? Imagine what she's thinking! Imagine your dismay if the toy breaks into sharp-edged pieces, the stuffed animal unravels and spills out crushed walnut hulls, a hinge pinches, or a battery shocks your child?

Children love toys for the fun and entertainment they provide. In addition, the playthings we give our sons and daughters can benefit them in important ways. Through playing with well-chosen toys, children can learn to focus their attention, can learn the laws of nature, can build positive self-esteem, and can express their creativity. Toys can also help them develop the skills they will need as adults. Our challenge as parents is to ensure that these benefits can be achieved safely and with lots of fun, too.

One of our greatest tendencies as parents is to rush to give a child an object that we enjoyed as children, without considering whether the child is mature enough to enjoy it safely. One such object is a balloon—a decorating item which encourages kids to kick and bat and giggle and wonder about its "magic" properties as it floats through the air. Balloons and babies, however, can be a deadly combination. Balloons break into small pieces just the right size to block the windpipe of the child who was biting it; balloon strings or ribbons can get twisted tightly around a child's finger or neck; a child may chase a balloon into the street. Fortunately, balloon packages usually are labeled,"Not Suitable For Children Under 3 Years; Close Supervision Required for Children 3 to 5 Years." As parents, we must routinely check for manufacturer's voluntary age recommendations. These warnings are generally sound and are intended to protect younger children from toys that have small parts, break relatively easily, or for some other reason aren't safe for youngsters under the stated age.

Even a reasonably well-made toy may break eventually, as a child pushes, pulls, or drops it, or tries to take it apart. Before giving a toy to a toddler, tug gently at attached parts to test their strength; flex a plastic toy slightly to test for brittleness or ease of breaking. Continue to check your child's toys regularly to make sure that they are still safe.

Be sure to give your child the supervision and guidance his age requires. Children up to the age of two require extremely close, almost constant, supervision. Between the ages of two and four, children are the most susceptible to toy-related injuries and continue to require close supervision. From this age on, boys are statistically more likely than girls to have accidents. Safety training can begin by teaching toddlers not to walk or run with things in their mouths and can continue as you train your growing preschooler to keep his toys with small parts away from the new baby.

Children play to learn, to grow, and to experience the world around them. Let's keep them safe while allowing them to build their self-esteem playing with age-appropriate toys.

Elise H. Ragland is an Educational Consultant and Senior Manager with Discovery Toys.

Outdoor Play

by James Talbot

If you're like a lot of caring and conscientious parents, you probably wish your yard offered a more stimulating atmosphere for your children. You've decided it's time to do something about it, but where to begin? Probably the first considerations that parents have to face about outdoor play sets are price and usefulness. You don't want one that breaks the budget, and yet you know that most swing sets offer mostly "exercise play," rather than challenging the imagination.

Self-directed play is the primary way children learn about themselves and the world in the early years. And children seek variety, change, challenge—even danger—in their play areas. Exercise-type play is required, but so is dramatic play, construction play, and games with rules. Here are some helpful guidelines to develop your yard's play potential—on a shoestring!

1. Get inspiration from books before starting. Read at least one book on play spaces and play design.

2. Walk a mile in their little shoes. Pay attention to children's patterns of play, noting which activities turn them on and sustain their attention. Remember your own past. Visit playgrounds and places interesting to them around town. Ask friends for recommendations.

3. Work with what's there. The next step is to assess your yard's resources. Do you have any trees? Is there a horizontal branch for a swing, or can a cantilevered beam be added? Is there a pair of trees to span an overhead beam between? Is there a cluster that might support a platform or treehouse? If a tree is structurally sound (even some dead trees are useable) and as big around as your arm, it is a candidate.

4. Do you have the right stuff? Loose parts are indispensable. Play needs props to be really fun: toys, bedspreads, kitchen utensils, blocks, barrels, wheeled toys, and hauling devices, crates, hay bales, old steering wheels, boards, boxes, spools, plywood, fabric, bamboo, rope, branches, carpeting, sawhorses, buckets, tubing—anything you happen to run across is fine that you think will spark their imaginations and that you deem safe. The spirit of recycling is ecologically sound, appropriate to play, and one that can be instilled at an early age.

5. Play it safe. Playspaces require safety inspections and routine maintenance. You can prevent accidents by becoming aware of their causes.

Falls to the ground or onto equipment are the biggest offenders. Use adequate railings and numerous easy-to-grasp hand holds. Always have a thick layer of sand or pea gravel under all fall zones. Make tall structures wide at the bottom and stepping in towards the top to avoid long free-falls, and keep the tops of all concrete footings well below the original dirt level. Opt for softer surfaces whenever you have a choice. Tires, which are resilient yet tough, can often be used in lieu of harder (and more expensive) materials. If there's no place set aside just for the children, then they'll always be in the wrong place. On the other hand, it's not that hard to turn your yard into a great place for those "wouldn't it be neat if" activities.

James Talbot is an architect and longtime builder and designer of Neverland Play Designs in Austin.

Capturing Childhood Moments on Film

by Gray Hawn

Even though I have been a professional photographer for many years, I did not realize how precious my family albums were to me until they were lost in a fire. What I miss most is being able to look through them and see my grandparents, my parents, myself, and my children when we were young. Seeing those photographs gave me a very special feeling that somehow I was in the childhood of my family. Because I have learned the importance of the special link between generations that is created by capturing childhood memories on film, I was delighted to be asked to write this article.

Photographing children captures much more than just images and feelings. The professional photographer captures those moments of shared emotion and caring that you will view later and remember the wonderful experience you had the day of the sitting. The art of great photography is to preserve those moments of sharing so that they may be relived over the years and never be forgotten. Children see the sun, moon, cloud puffs, and stars and respond to them with innocence and awe. Such is the magic of the child's world. If we are to capture that world on film, we must set our "grownupness" aside and discover, with them, the laughter of the wind and the wonder of the dancing of the leaves. For children, the rhythms that lie just below the surface of existence are gentle and loving. If we would truly enter their world and capture their spirit, we must allow the rhythms of our own lives to come into harmony with theirs.

I believe that every parent that can should own a camera. If you visit any large camera store, you will find a compact, fully automatic camera (including automatic focus). Buy it! Then when you get home, practice picking it up and shooting quickly, so when your child takes those first steps or splatters Grandmother with baby food, you will be able to save the experience forever.

Another way to capture childhood moments is to hire a professional photographer. A question I often hear goes something like, "Why should I hire someone when Uncle Harry just bought that fancy camera?" To answer that, I will share with you what I think professional photography can accomplish.

The areas in which professional photographers should offer more than you can accomplish on your own are image, composition, color, spirit, interactions, and artistry.

Thought and creativity are far more important than a floor plan of lighting positions with children. Portraits should be compassionate, gentle, and personal. The photographer must be able to relate and respond intuitively to the child's sense of spontaneity. Professional photographers spend a lifetime learning their techniques. They excel technically. They know mood, feeling, and posing. They understand lighting, composition, exposure factor, and all the necessary controls to create an image on film. Their cameras must become extensions of their arms so that their minds will be free to relate to the subject as they create their photography, and their feelings will be free to make the experience enjoyable to those they photograph. As photographers master all of these abilities, they develop a unique and original style of their own.

Now that you know what professional photographers try to do, I will list the three types of professional photography that work with children.

The first is studio photography. Studio photography is done at a fixed inside location. Sittings last from a few minutes to over an hour. Prices range from less than $20 in some department stores to hundreds of dollars at "name" studios.

The second is portrait photography. Portrait photographers work both in their studios and in natural settings, such as Zilker Gardens, and in their clients' homes. Sittings last from a few minutes in their studios to two hours or longer on location. Sitting fees begin at around $50 and prices for a typical print can vary from $10 to $100.

The third is master photography. I use the term "master" to refer to the quality of the photographer's work rather than to any kind of professional degree. Master photographers are full-time professionals. Besides working with their clients, they attend professional conventions, keep up with the latest developments in photographic technology, and enter their work in professional competition where it is judged and criticized by their peers. They know that true photographic artists never stop learning.

Before selecting a photographer, you should decide how you want your child photographed. Do you want a sitting in a studio, in your home, or in an outdoor setting? How do you want your child dressed, formally or informally? If you are in a studio, do you want a dark or a high-key white background? If you are in your home, do you want artificial lighting or window lighting? If you are outdoors, do you want an action or a posed photograph? Or do you want the photographer to create something unique and different?

If you decide to use a professional photographer, how do you find one that will suit your needs? First, ask your friends. If they have someone they were pleased with and you like the photographer's work and prices, go with their recommendation. If your friends cannot help, select the type of work and photographer you want from the ideas above, decide what you want to spend, and start calling. Do not be afraid to ask what the fees and print prices are. Ask where they learned photography and what degrees or honors they have earned. If you want outdoor work, ask how many rolls of film they shoot (the more the better). Then, when you have narrowed your list to two or three, visit their studios and see their work. Be sure to meet them to see if you like them. And finally, always remember: good photographers like people and love their work; great photographers love both.

Photography is a place where time stops and golden moments live forever, a place where children and butterflies and rainbows never age or fly away or fade, a place to which we can always return.

Gray Hawn is an internationally renowned photographer.

Albert M. Tate, Jr., D.D.S., M.S.D., Pediatric Dentistry

As a specialist in pediatric dentistry, Dr. Bert Tate practices early intervention to prevent cavities and interceptive orthodontics to guide growth and development of the jaws. Patients range from teething age through high school age. Dr. Tate has been in practice in Austin since 1969. A graduate of Baylor University, Waco, and Baylor College of Dentistry, Dallas, Dr. Tate completed an additional two-year residency to specialize in Pediatric Dentistry.

Dr. Tate strives to make dentistry as much fun as possible, creating a relaxed atmosphere and stressing the importance of taking care of the teeth. The patients are treated as friends. He likes to see children early, around nine to twelve months, and offers a free exam to children under three years. Parent education is an important part of the practice. The office accepts MasterCard and Visa, as well as offering flexible payment plans and accepting most dental insurance plans.

Albert M. Tate, Jr., D.D.S., M.S.D. • 11111 Research Blvd., Suite 395 • 338-5151
1305 W. 34th St., Suite 208 • 452-8283 • Hours by appointment

Raymond K. Oukrop, D.D.S.

Dr. Oukrop is a graduate of the University of Iowa and the Iowa College of Dentistry. He has practiced in Wyoming and Texas for more than 28 years. At Walter Reed Army Hospital, he worked with Robert Shira, D.D.S., the past president of the American Dental Association who made major innovative contributions to modern dentistry. Dr. Oukrop works with patients ranging from three years to senior citizens. He offers a full range of family dentistry, cosmetic dentistry, and interceptive orthodontics to correct problems and, in some cases, prevent full orthodontic correction later. He strives to get to know his patients personally and has a genuine concern for their well-being and comfort during and after treatment. He uses non-toxic materials for fillings.

Raymond K. Oukrop, D.D.S.
609 Castle Ridge Road (Bee Caves Rd. at 360) • 327-5977
Office Open Monday — Thursday, 8:30-4; Friday, 8-12

Austin Regional Clinic - Ear/Nose/Throat
Richard Denton, M.D., Stephen Mitchell, M.D.,
Stephen Muller, M.D. • Associates in Otolaryngology
1301 West 38th Street, Suite 401 • 458-4276

David S. Wishnew, M.D.

Dr. David Wishnew graduated from Clark University in Worchester, Mass. with a B.A. in psychology. He did graduate work in child psychology at New School for Social Research in New York and attended medical school at the University of Brussels in Belgium. He studied General Surgery in Buffalo, New York and did his residency in Plastic Surgery at Buffalo General Hospital and Buffalo Children's Hospital. He has been in practice since 1984.

Dr. Wishnew does plastic surgery on congenital and acquired deformities and trauma, including burns, facial injuries, body lacerations, and hand injuries. Having been trained in child psychology, Dr. Wishnew is able to build up a level of trust with the child, which is especially helpful in a trauma situation. He also offers a full range of cosmetic and reconstructive surgery. Dr. Wishnew is active in the Austin Smiles program, a non-profit organization that provides expertise on a volunteer basis for children in many third-world nations who suffer from cleft lip or cleft palate and have no hope locally for treatment.

David S. Wishnew, M.D.
4007 James Casey C-250 • 440-1555
11645 Angus Road, Suite 8 • 343-2553

"As we contemplate the miracle of birth, as we renew in our hearts the sense of wonder and joy, may we be stirred to a fresh awareness of the sacredness of life and of the divine promise of childhood. May we so live that all our children will be able to acquire our best virtues and to leave behind our worst failings. May we pass on the light of courage and compassion, and the questing spirit; and may that light burn more brightly in these our children than it has in us."
—Robert Marshall

Discovery Toys®
Developmental Toys, Books & Games for ages birth to adult
Elise Ragland, Educational Consultant & Sr. Manager • 478-1872
Call for info. on in-home demonstrations or business opportunity

Create A Rainbow

• Educational Toys
• Books & Tapes

Lake Hills Plaza
4211 South Lamar A-27

(512) 445-5437
Austin, Texas 78704

Create A Rainbow

Angelita Dominguez, a former special-education teacher and educational diagnostician, has ventured and become the new owner of Create A Rainbow as of July, 1989. She and her associates are working hard at creating an environment that is exciting and educational to children.

Create A Rainbow carries durable quality toys from Brio, Playmobil, and Ambi. You will also find a wide selection of dolls, including Gotz, Robin Woods, Ginny, and Petra. A new line of dollhouses and accessories will also be introduced.

The Resource Room includes an extensive selection of books, teaching aides, record albums, video tapes, and audio tapes. You will also find a wide variety of games, puzzles, puppets, manipulatives, arts and crafts, science kits, and a "make-believe" section.

Create A Rainbow has built its reputation on its selection of educational and developmental toys, books, and tapes. But the selections are not just educational—they are also fun and entertaining, and sure to bring a smile to the face of your favorite child.

Feel free to bring your child along when you shop. Create A Rainbow has a "hands-on" play area for children to try out toys and entertain themselves while you shop.

The goal of Create A Rainbow is to foster your child's creativity, coordination, and cognitive development through fun and interesting play.

Create A Rainbow accepts MasterCard and Visa. It also offers the following services: gift wrapping, UPS shipping, layaway, and phone orders.

Create A Rainbow
4211 S. Lamar, Suite A-27
445-5437
Open Monday - Saturday, 10 am — 5:30 pm

Back•In•A•Flash

If you want your treasured photos back fast, back safe, and back as good as they can be, you want to leave your color print film with Back•In•A•Flash. Photofinishing in-house means that your film never leaves the location where you drop it off. The photo lab is in the store so your color print film is never lost in shipping from one place to another. The people who process your film are specialists—they don't do anything but work with photographs, so you can be sure that they will treat your pictures with care and expertise.

Seven locations in Austin offer color prints, color slides, color enlargements, black-and-white prints, color prints from slides, color laser copies, and commercial pickup and delivery.

Five of the studios (Oak Hill, Balcones, Northcross, Lakehills, and Highland) offer a portrait studio, and all offer instant passport photos. The photographers who work for Back•In•A•Flash are all trained professionals who will have your proofs ready for you to look at within one hour and your final prints ready the next day. Normally, you don't need to plan ahead and make appointments for a time in the future when you may have a runny nose. You can drop by the studio and have your portrait done at a low cost and at your convenience, but calling for an appointment will ensure that you won't have to wait. Picture frames are also available at the studios so that in one 24-hour period you can have a beautifully framed portrait of your family or your child ready to display. Back•In•A•Flash portraits are perfect for keeping up with your ever-changing youngster. The cost is so low that you can have many packages for the price of one at other studios. The basic portrait package includes two 8x10s, four 5x7s, and nine wallets or sixteen miniwallets, and costs only $29.99.

An Austin-owned business since 1980, Back•In•A•Flash has grown because of its excellent services. In addition, it serves the community by supporting the Children's Hospital at Brackenridge, March of Dimes, Muscular Dystrophy, YMCA, Aqua Fest, Arthritis Foundation, and Big Brothers/Big Sisters of Austin. All locations accept Visa, MasterCard, Discover, and American Express.

Back•In•A•Flash
Specializing in Children's Portraits
Lakehills Plaza • 447-4403, South Lamar & Ben White Blvd.
Oak Hill Plaza • 288-4770, at the "Y"
915 N. Lamar • 474-8338, Business District
5212 N. Lamar • 452-8144, North Business District
Highland Mall • 451-7593, Airport Blvd. at Koenig Ln.
Northcross Mall • 452-2501, Burnet Rd. at W. Anderson Ln.
Balcones Woods • 346-3598, 11150 Research Blvd.

Prints Charming Photography

Take a close look at the front and back covers of this book. These photographs were taken by Jane Steig Parsons of Prints Charming Photography. Her ability to capture the essence of what makes each child special is quickly evident. She records the uniqueness of the moment—be it a child's playfulness, the bond between a human and a pet, the flavor of a relationship, or the meaning of an event. She moves beyond the narrow confines of the studio into natural, personally meaningful settings to create works of unusual freshness and integrity.

For 20 years Jane has created expressive candid portraits of children in their own environments—absorbed in an activity, interacting with family members, lost in thought, playing "dress up," loving a pet, or happily covered in mud. The skills and attitudes important in her former careers as educational psychologist and elementary teacher help establish the rapport needed to produce attractive and spontaneous expressions.

In 1983 Jane established Prints Charming Photography, and her clientele was extended to include brides, families, models, actors, job-seekers, and other individuals and businesses. Prints Charming Photography currently photographs weddings, receptions, birthdays, anniversaries, and other special occasions, as well as commercial work for publicity purposes. You can find Jane's photographs in the brochures and advertisements of Austin medical practitioners, psychologists, individual business people, and both profit and non-profit organizations.

Prints Charming Photography also offers some less easily obtainable photographic services: custom color post cards for holiday greetings, retouching of prints and negatives, selective color, and restoration of old photographs.

Jane holds memberships in national, state, and local professional photography organizations. Her work has appeared in books, calendars, newspapers, and magazines, such as *Parenting in the '90s* (cover), the *Senior's Guide to Austin* (cover), the Book of Days Calendar, *Austin American-Statesman, West Austin News, Austin Citizen, Austin Chronicle, the Advocate, Austin Family Magazine, Austin Woman,* and the *American Way Magazine.*

She has also exhibited widely in Austin galleries, bookstores, restaurants, medical offices, pet establishments, and other businesses, among them the Texas Photographic Gallery, The Alternate Space Gallery, Bank of the Hills, and First Federal Savings. Currently her work is on display at the Prints Charming Gallery and in more than a dozen other Austin businesses.

Prints Charming Photography brochures, price lists, client references, and a list of locations exhibiting Jane Parsons' photographs are available upon request.

Prints Charming Photography
9001 Laurel Grove Drive • 836-2514

About Images Photography

Mary Wasmuth offers a full-service photography studio, including passport pictures, wedding photography, and restoration of old or damaged photographs. Her favorite subject, however, is children. She offers photography sessions both in the studio and on location. She believes in natural photography, capturing the subject in natural rather than artificial poses, and lets her customers assist in creating their own portraits. Children are constantly changing expressions and poses. Mary captures this variety and delight of your child and preserves his or her unique charm in a way that can be treasured for a lifetime. An informal, relaxed approach to photography makes the subjects feel more comfortable and makes the experience fun.

Mary Wasmuth began photography as a hobby, but the hobby soon developed into a full-time business in 1980. She is a member of the Professional Photographers Guild of Austin, Texas Professional Photographers Association, and Professional Photographers of America; she has received awards from the local association and in 1988 won second place as Photographer of the Year. The hours of the studio are flexible, and MasterCard, American Express, and Visa are accepted.

About Images Photography
13376 Research Blvd. #500 • 250-8339
Call for Appointment

Gray Hawn & Associates

Gray Hawn & Associates takes photography from a level of capturing a specific image to an art form. Each photograph is something poetic—a fleeting moment to last a lifetime. The goal is to create something different which goes beyond the surface to capture the soul and feelings of the subjects. The studio works with children, families, and individuals to create portraits of depth and sensitivity. They especially enjoy photographing mothers and babies together, capturing the love and caring in the relationship. Weddings, commercial work, executive portraits, brochures, magazine covers, and other subjects are done with style and grace.

An artist for many years, Gray began photographing 13 years ago. She works in the U.S. and Europe. She has photographed such celebrities as Sophia Loren, Farah Fawcett, Earl Campbell, Jimmy Carter, and Lady Bird Johnson. She created the last portrait of Princess Grace of Monaco. In his book, Jack Curtis said of her work, "In the future we may look back on her renaissance style and impressionistic feeling and recognize it as a whole new school of photography." The photographer accepts MasterCard and Visa and is available by appointment.

Gray Hawn & Associates
P.O. Box 162425 • Austin 78716 • 328-1321

"A baby is not like a picture that you hang on the wall and enjoy forever afterward. A baby is not even like a house which, once secured, must be kept up, or the roof will leak, the paint peel off, and the plumbing give out. A baby, more than anything else in the world, will grow and develop in accordance with what you do or do not do; in accordance with the devotion and the intelligence, the courage and the patience you bring to the task of caring for him.

"With a newborn baby, the potential for good or ill is so great, new parents sometimes feel virtually crushed by the weight of it. They know their own shortcomings. They know their ignorance. They know their frailties, their psychological problems, and all the other weaknesses to which human flesh is heir. They know that, resolve as they will to do their best, they will not always do it. They know they will be angry, thoughtless, intemperate, vindictive, and, more often than they suspect, ignorant of their own motives, unconsciously, even self-righteously, taking out on their children, the frustrations from which they themselves suffer.

"So we are possessed by a sense of obligation, of purpose, and of determination, that we shall be worthy of the gift that has been given into our hands."

—Duncan Howlett

CHAPTER III

The Preschool Years

(3-5 years)

by Patrice Davis, Grade 3, Langford Elementary

Evaluating Your Child's Development

by Susan McMillan, Ph.D.

The basic categories of development are biological, cognitive, emotional, and personal-social. Biological development concerns itself with increased motor control and maturation and growth of the body. Cognitive development includes not only the intellectual and problem-solving skills, but also how the child comes to comprehend the outer world or physical environment. Sometimes language development is included as part of the overall cognitive processes. Three to six is a time for the who, where, why, how, and when questions. This progression represents the increasing complexity of the concepts underlying the questions. Emotional or personality development refers to a child's intrapsychic growth as reflected in his interpersonal behavior and the affective experiences—love, hate, anger, fear, anxiety. Feelings also result from interactions with other people; therefore, there is a link between social experience and development of emotions and self. Personal-social development is shaped in accordance with goals held by the family and society.

The overall process of development can be seen in the occurrences of stages and segments of behavior. At each stage there are certain problems to be solved and when a child succeeds or masters these, he goes on to tackle new problems and grows through solving them. These problems are often called the tasks of that stage of childhood. The specific developmental tasks of the preschool child are: growth of self-awareness, attainment of some degree of emotional control, movement from preoperational to intuitive cognitive development, formation of the concepts of good and bad with the appearance of the conscience, learning social communication in the peer group, and learning and identification of appropriate sex role.

One might think of this time period as one of understanding, planning, and attacking the world. The problems of this age are literally played out in the world of imagination and make-believe. Developmental stages are generally named after the activities that the child carries on during that period (See Table 1).

The preschool years are significant for both personality and cognitive growth. With the sense of autonomy well in hand, the sense of initiative and imagination becomes the main focus for the preschool child. Although he thinks concretely, his imagination takes him far and wide. The preschool child explores everything—places, people, language, objects, art material. And with and through this exploration he starts new activities and gets new ideas. He can also create the experience he wants, trying on the role of mother or father or doctor, contemplating what adults do, imagining how it would be if he himself were doing it. Most vital of all are the roles of his parents. These are the parts he plays most often, especially that of the parent of the same sex. If his seeking is successful, then he finds a wide variety of things he can do, make, and create with the approval of his family and other adults.

Aggression is also part of initiative since it involves pushing out into the world and attacking. Conscience begins to develop at this time, regulating initiative and imagination. The child takes the voice of his parents into himself, saying what is all right to do or not do. If he does not obey he may feel guilty. He may even feel guilty for thoughts or wishes. His imagination may hit or kill people who anger him or may create a monster to eat the annoying people. This magical thinking is particularly powerful if an outer event happens to coincide with the thought. Parents must achieve a balance between encouragement of initiative and consistent transmission of a sense of right and wrong. It is important that parents model the ethics they attempt to instill in their offspring because the cognitive ability of the child now allows him to distinguish between what the parents do and what they say.

During the period of time when initiative dominates, it is more important to start things than to finish them. Achievement or finishing things and doing well becomes more important in the stage that follows. However, the attitude that his parents take toward his exploration and new activities lays the foundation for later achievement.

The play of the preschool child takes cognitive, imaginative, and motor activities and weaves them together. Through play the child integrates developing intellectual activity and then explores the boundaries of his competencies. Play is also the way a child this age deals with his troubles and insecurities. For example, he can pretend to be big and powerful by being superman or a policeman. Play helps with painful experiences or with troubling situations such as surgeries or birth of a sibling. Many hospitals have specific play programs set up to help the child work through the fears, anxieties, and anger that come with an operation or a long hospital stay. Play helps the child to feel stronger and more confident and to work out specific uncomfortable feelings. Play for this age child is his work.

Table I
Cognitive

0-1 year—Sensory motor intelligence—Achievement is for baby to know environment as permanent objects and background, separate from self.

1-3 years—Preoperation—Symbolic functions, language, symbolic play. Internalization of actions into thoughts. Group objects together, define the nature of the categories, and learn relationships between them.

3-6 years—Intuitive—More or less beads? More because higher. Type of thought activity is irreversible: A to B but not B to A
Ball of clay rolled out more, roll back to original, unable to see.

Personality

0-1 year—Development of Trust vs Mistrust
Able to tolerate temporary parental absence

1-3 years—Autonomy vs Shame and Doubt
Sense of autonomy built on trust—for as child comes to control objects, his own body, and people, he comes to realize that he can cause certain events and can choose to do or not to do. Learns self-assertion.

3-6 years—Imitative and Imagination vs Guilt
Child explores world of people and things, imagines himself in a variety of roles, seeks answers, solutions, and new ideas if he can do, make, and create with approval of family and friends. Aggression and assertive behavior, pushing out, and attacking. Development of conscience. Broadens skills and learns cooperation, begins to become independent.

Susan McMillan is a Pediatric Psychologist.

Coping with Allergies in Infants and Children

by Larry James, M.D.

Allergic illness in infants and young children can be especially frustrating for parents. I see many small children in my practice, and a common complaint is, "The baby is always congested. He has had many ear infections, his nose is always stuffy, and we can't get him off antibiotics." Such problems can be stressful on the family, as well as a financial burden, since one parent, usually the mother, must miss work to take the baby to the pediatrician, pay for the office visit, and buy medication. A single episode may cost $100 or more. In many such cases, allergic sensitivities are the main cause of the chronic illness.

It is possible to make a reasonably accurate estimate of the cause or causes of an infant's or young child's allergic problems based on the child's age. In the first two years of life, a food, usually cow's milk, causes most allergy problems. A diet free of milk usually corrects the chronic congestion. Many baby foods contain milk so they should be avoided. Fortunately, many others do not contain milk, and an adequate variety is available after eliminating milk products. Milk substitutes are used in place of cow's milk formulas. Often a soy-based formula is used, but it may also cause problems because soy protein is very allergenic. Goat's milk is not a good substitute for the same reason. Protein hydrolysate formulas are the least allergenic and usually the best alternative.

As the infant grows into childhood and horizons are broadened, new allergens begin to play a role in the child's allergic problems. Around age two, indoor inhalants (air-borne) begin to cause problems, especially house dust mites and indoor pets. As a general rule, an indoor pet should never be around an allergic child. Mattress and pillow casings, air filters, and tannic acid spray help in controlling mite exposure.

Mold spore sensitivity usually does not develop until age three, and seasonal pollen sensitivity develops around age four. These are generalizations, but allergic sensitivities develop only after adequate repeated exposures, and the order noted above correlates with the amount of exposure a child has as he grows.

What can be done? First, don't believe that nothing can be done, and don't accept the statement: "There's nothing to worry about. Your child will outgrow this." While this may be true in some cases, it may be 12 or more years before the problems are outgrown. If both parents have allergy problems, there is a 60 percent chance that their children will also. It has been suggested that conception should be planned so that the baby is born in the early summer when colds and other infections are low and airborne allergens are low. During pregnancy, the mother should avoid highly allergenic foods such as milk, eggs, and peanuts. After the baby is born, breastfeeding should be used for at least nine months. Use hypoallergenic formulas for supplemental feedings and avoid baby foods that contain milk. While breastfeeding, the mother should remain on a hypo-allergenic diet. There should be no indoor pets, and there should be no tobacco smoking in the house. If a child with allergy problems or potential allergy problems must attend day care, choose a private home with no more than five children, no smokers, and no indoor pets.

These methods are not perfect, but on the average they have been shown to lessen the severity of allergic problems and delay their onset. If you try these and your child still has chronic problems, allergy skin tests should be considered. (Note: Much has been said and written about blood tests for allergies. These are often negative when skin tests are positive, so they should be used only when skin tests are not possible. Blood tests for allergic sensitivities are also more expensive than skin tests.) If skin testing suggests sensitivites to allergens that cannot be avoided, allergy injections to decrease the child's sensitivity could be tried. If allergy injections are used, improvement can occur within three to six months. If no improvement is seen after one year of treatment, allergy injections should be discontinued. If improvement *is* seen, they should be given for at least four years, and the interval between the injections should be gradually increased until the child is receiving one injection monthly and needing very little, if any, medication. Once this goal is achieved and the injections have been given for at least four years, they may be stopped with little concern for a relapse of symptoms.

Asthma is the most significant allergic disease. It may begin at any age and may have many degrees of severity. Fortunately, with modern medications, avoidance, and allergy injections, asthma can be controlled.

It is important to remember that your child does not need to be congested all the time. You do not need to be treating ear and sinus infections or bronchitis every two to four weeks. Such problems often can be prevented by appropriate avoidance of allergens, proper use of medications, and sometimes allergy injections.

Larry James is an allergy and asthma specialist.

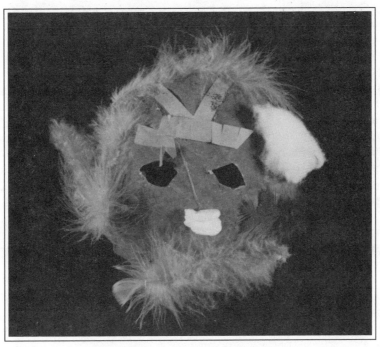

by Chris Rorie, age 4, Phoenix School

The Importance of a Good Eye Exam

by Lonn Bradley Lockhart, M.D.

When should your child have his or her first eye examination? That question often comes up during the preschool years. Actually, your child has already had at least one eye examination. Your pediatrician examined his or her eyes during the newborn checkup. All pediatricians are trained to evaluate babies for eye problems that occur shortly after birth.

Probably a better question to ask during the preschool years is when should your child's vision be tested? A visual acuity, the 20/20 or 20/30 type numbered measurement of vision, should be checked at around age three. Of course, few three year olds are going to sit up and read the regular letter chart. Your three year old, however, should be able to respond to picture cards and picture charts that are designed for his or her age group. Vision should be tested this early because most vision loss is much more effectively treated when it is found at an early age. School vision-screening programs usually do a good job of detecting vision loss. A child, however, may get his or her first school screen at age six or seven. If he or she has had visual loss since age two or three, it might be too late to recover vision.

If your child has blurry vision, he or she will probably not complain about it. Many children just assume that the world is fuzzy because it has always been that way. Or vision can very gradually become blurry, and the change is not noticed. If only one eye is blurry, your child may not notice that either.

There are, however, several things that you can watch for. Squinting may be a sign that your child cannot see well. Some children sit close to the TV because they like to. Other children get close because they must to see. If your child must get close, have his or her vision checked.

One of your child's eyes may not appear straight. It may seem to drift in toward the nose, out away from the nose, or even up or down. If this occurs briefly during the first few months of life, it is probably normal. If it continues anytime after age six months, it may be a sign of visual loss. Another sign of poor vision may be squinting of just one eye. Also, comparing one eye to the other is useful. If one eye doesn't look quite like the other, in any way, this should be checked out. Early treatment of a wandering eye is very effective. Treatment postponed for years does not help.

Most children who need glasses get their first pair in early grade school. Usually this is because a school screening program has detected a visual problem. Your child may need glasses at any age. Nearsightedness means that things that are close appear clear. Things far away are blurry. Nearsightedness can develop at any age. Glasses should be prescribed when your child's vision becomes blurry enough to interfere with his or her activities and learning. Some two year olds need glasses. Some twenty-year-old adults finally need their first pair.

Your child may have one eye that is normal, while the other eye needs a strong glasses prescription. This is hard to detect without a vision test. It needs to be treated, though, at age three to four years. The eye can then develop normally and vision loss will only be temporary.

Eye injuries are too common and usually preventable. Seatbelts and child restraining seats definitely decrease the risk of eye damage in car accidents. Restraints should always be worn. Most eye injuries occur when the eye is struck with a fast-moving object, such as a BB or rock. Parental supervision is essential, particularly if preschool children are in range. Sharp objects of any kind can also do damage if placed in the wrong hands. Eye injuries from baseballs are rare in preschool years. These are more likely to occur in older children when ball velocity is much greater. Hockey face guards and, recently, baseball eye shields have saved many eyes. If your child is struck severely in the eye, open the eye gently and look in. If you see something that does not appear normal, call your doctor. Don't touch the eye until you have been advised.

It's important to know who's who in eyecare so that you can choose the best professional to check your child's eyes. An optician is a person who fits glasses or contact lenses based on a prescription that is brought in by you. That prescription must be obtained from an optometrist or an ophthalmologist. An optometrist is a doctor of optometry who is trained and licensed to examine eyes, fit and prescribe glasses and contact lenses, and treat some eye problems. An ophthalmologist is a doctor of medicine who is trained and licensed to examine eyes, fit and prescribe glasses and contact lenses, and treat all eye problems visually, medically, or surgically. If you have a problem deciding who to see, ask your child's doctor.

Lonn Bradley Lockhart is a pediatric ophthalmologist, a Diplomate American Board of Ophthalmology, and Fellow American Academy of Ophthalmology.

by Julian Pruneda, age 10, Austin Montessori School

Finding the Preschool to Meet Your Needs

by Rhonda Paver

Finding the preschool to meet your needs can be a difficult and time-consuming task. In general, there are several variables to consider while searching for child care.

First, it is important to start early in your search. Many schools have waiting lists, so it is important to get a start while you have time to spare.

When visiting preschools, look into the philosophy of the program. In general, schools fall into several categories. The traditional approach to early childhood education incorporates a view that encompasses the development of the entire child. This approach advocates learning in an environment that meets the emotional, physical, social, and cognitive needs of the child. Specifically, the meeting of these needs is achieved in the following ways:

Emotional needs of children are nurtured by warm and caring staff who strive to make children feel secure and special. Staff help children to be successful throughout the day by giving frequent praise and encouragement. Creativity and self-expression are encouraged through activities and an atmosphere in which children's thoughts and ideas are valued.

Physical development is encouraged through activities which develop large and small muscle coordination. These include puzzles, manipulative toys, art, creative movement, and outdoor play.

Social development is encouraged via opportunities to be with other children under the guidance of trained teachers. Children learn to share, take turns, and cooperate as they work and play together.

Cognitive development is encouraged through activities which promote exploration, problem solving, and experimentation.

Programs should work with the knowledge that young children are active learners. They learn through doing. Activities should be planned around units of study that are meaningful and interesting to young children.

Parents should look for learning centers throughout the school. Children have the opportunity to work and play in these centers by choice. The centers should contain educational toys, teaching games, and materials that the children may use individually, with a friend, or in small groups. Centers provide practice in making decisions, following directions, working independently, and learning the care and use of materials.

Programs available to parents include Montessori, private, corporate, and church-related programs. Within the framework of these programs, many services are available to parents. These might include full- and part-time programs, two- or three-day-per-week programs, after-school programs, and summer programs. Many churches offer a "mother's day out" program which can meet the needs very successfully of those with less-demanding work schedules.

Parents should discuss a full range of services with the directors of the programs they visit. Important questions to ask include the hours of operation, nutritional information, curriculum guidelines, and teacher training. Many centers are also willing to give references to help parents make better informed decisions.

Parental visits should be encouraged at the center. It is important that parents feel they are welcome at all times, and an "open door" policy should be encouraged. Some form of daily communication should exist between teachers and parents. This may be a written note, a brief conversation, or some other convenient form of communication. The center should provide support to parents through a number of avenues. These might include a monthly newsletter, a parent education program, or a lending or reading library. Certain video tapes are also available for the purpose of parent education.

Parents should also be encouraged to check the history of the center with the Department of Human Resources. They will receive information about complaints. If complaints exist, parents should feel free to discuss these with the center director. Parents should also be encouraged to look at two or three schools before choosing a place for their child.

Early childhood education programs can have a positive effect on the development of young children. Parents will want to consider the individual needs of their child before deciding on a program. Children thrive in an environment that is well suited to their individual personality. Parents should always be positive about their child's participation in an early-childhood program. The attitude conveyed by the parent is passed along to the child and helps the child with a smooth transition to a new situation.

Rhonda Paver is the owner and executive director of The Stepping Stone Child Development Centers.

by Elizabeth Wilborn, age 10, Austin Montessori School

Montessori: An Effective Alternative in Education

by Don and Donna Goertz

Montessori is more than a teaching method; it is a philosophy of life. It is based on the principle that each child is an individual with unique needs, interests and patterns of growth. The Montessori Method evolved from Dr. Maria Montessori's work with young children in the early 1900s. From her observations, Dr. Montessori devised methods and materials to be used in helping children of all capabilities to learn. She realized that the child literally absorbs information from the environment. When the environment is prepared for the child's exploration, and the teacher responds to the child's interests and needs within this environment, the child flourishes—experiencing learning as a limitless opportunity rather than a requirement.

The Montessori approach to education aims to ensure the natural development of the whole personality of the child, his physical and emotional faculties, as well as his intellectual powers. It offers the child a maximum of spontaneity in choice of physical and mental activity, whereby the child reaches the same or, more often, higher levels of scholastic attainment than under old, traditional systems.

The classroom

A Montessori classroom is typified by the soft hum of activity as the children busily go about their various tasks. They are free to move about the room and explore the rich and ordered environment which has been prepared for them and which offers a wide variety of colorful and attractive materials designed to lead them naturally and logically from concrete experiences to abstract ideas. They are free to work, experiment, and explore by themselves or in a way that blends harmoniously with the group. A large measure of liberty is allowed them based on respect for the rights of others. This presents endless opportunity for mutual work and help—joyfully given and received. It also eliminates the frustration and boredom of waiting for other children to learn, as well as the intimidation and discouragement of lagging behind others.

The classroom is a microcosmic society in which the children are grouped in three-year age spans rather than according to traditional grades. They learn in cooperation and develop social skills as they become responsible contributors to the group. The younger children benefit from the older ones' expertise, while the older children benefit, both intellectually and emotionally, from sharing with the younger ones. For example, a child may stop to observe another's work. This can provide learning for the observer and is respected as valuable.

Primary level (two and one-half to six years)

All subjects are approached as a movement from whole areas of study to detailed consideration of the parts. At the primary level (two and one-half to six year olds), Practical Life exercises and Sensorial materials are emphasized. An environment scaled to their size allows the children maximum self-sufficiency. This forms the foundation of their future development and education.

Practical Life exercises guide the children toward mastery of their environment, whereas Sensorial materials guide the children to utilize their five senses with a high degree of discrimination. The two and one-half to six year olds develop a strong intellectual foundation by working individually and in small groups with specially-designed materials for experiencing basic concepts of language, mathematics, geography, the sciences, and music.

Elementary level (six to twelve years)

At the elementary level, along with developmentally sequenced activities, the children are presented with the "Cosmic Curriculum," which teaches them the inter-relatedness of knowledge and the interdependencies of life through impressionistic stories on the formation and development of earth and the evolution of plant and animal life, as well as the development of man and the history of civilization. At about six years of age, children advance from the primary level to the lower elementary where they strive for mastery of skills in reading, writing, mathematics, life sciences, geography, history, music, art, and physical education. At around nine years of age, the students move into the upper elementary. With a strong foundation in basic skills and a broad cultural overview, the nine- to twelve-year-old students inquire more deeply into life sciences, advanced mathematics, grammar and composition, literature, world history, music, and art.

Just as in the primary level, special materials for all areas of curriculum are used at the elementary level. Computers, too, are utilized by the students as a tool to assist in various aspects of their studies. Education is not limited to the classroom and a single class group. As the child progresses into higher levels, the horizons of the learning environment are continually expanded. The children receive sound preparation for the real world, both in academic knowledge and in practical terms seldom addressed by traditional forms of education. The Montessori environment allows the children to acquire knowledge and to develop skills, while at the same time developing their individual character. This balance is integral to the unfolding of the Montessori method of education.

The children initiate and carry out projects in social responsibility related to the environment, world peace, community service, and social problems. They are encouraged to research, plan, and act independently and responsibly. Fundamental to Montessori is the belief that if the child is guided with love and understanding, his curiosity will lead him into a full education. He will develop fully, at his own pace, confident of his own abilities. He will become independent earlier. These concepts are not education idealism. They have been proven in Montessori classrooms throughout the world.

Donna Bryant Goertz is the founder of Austin Montessori School. Donald C. Goertz, Ph.D., is the executive director of Austin Montessori School.

Aero-Allergen Clinic

Dr. Russell R. Roby holds degrees in both law and medicine. He graduated from the University of Texas law school in 1964 and from the UT Medical School at San Antonio in 1973. He served on the Pediatric House Staff at Hermann Hospital in Houston and is a Fellow in the College of Legal Medicine and a member of the American Association for Clinical Immunology and Allergy. The clinic is dedicated to the diagnosis and treatment of allergies. A thorough examination and necessary tests begin the process of determining allergies. Treatment depends on the substance to which the patient is allergic. Sometimes substances can be avoided; in other cases, immunotherapy is prescribed to help the patient build up immunity to the offending substances. Dr. Roby uses a five-part approach to each patient: medical, physical, nutritional, supplemental, and attitudinal. Dr. Roby has an ongoing program to help patients deal with allergies. He recommends prescription drugs when necessary in addition to diet, exercise, record-keeping, vitamins, and other techniques. Dr. Roby seeks to treat the whole individual—both the person and his environment. Dr. Roby has also worked extensively with food allergies and candida, both difficult to manage.

Aero-Allergen Clinic• 3410 Far West Blvd., Suite 110 • 338-4336
Office open 8 am - 5 pm, Monday - Friday

Austin Regional Clinic - Allergy Treatment & Testing
William R. Otto, M.D., Board Certified in Allergy/Immunology
1600 West 38th Street, Suite 300 • 371-5401

Larry James, M.D. • Allergy & Asthma Care for Children
11770 Jollyville Rd. • 331-5118
1305 West 34th • 467-1164
13409 Burnet Rd. • 244-7161

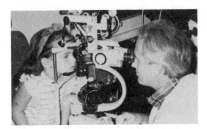

O.B. Jackson, Jr., M.D., F.A.C.S.

Dr. Jackson's practice focuses on pediatric ophthalmology (medical and surgical diseases of the eye) with emphasis on lazy eye, droopy eyelid, and other eye muscle imbalances in all ages, as well as tear duct obstruction, infantile cataracts, acute eye injuries, eye infections, glasses, and contact lenses. He opened his practice in 1976 after undergraduate work at Texas Tech, an internship at John Peter Smith Hospital in Ft. Worth, residency at Parkland Memorial Hospital in Dallas, and a fellowship in Pediatric Ophthalmology at the University of Iowa. Dr. Jackson is a member of the American Association of Pediatric Ophthalmology and Strabismus, Special Fellow of the American Academy of Pediatrics, and Fellow of the American College of Surgeons. His research has led to various publications and, establishment of the research labs in saccadic velocity at Seton Medical Center and in oculinum injection at Bailey Square Surgical Center. Dr. Jackson works with the Austin Pediatric Education Program at Brackenridge Hospital and is a faculty member at the University of Texas Medical Branch in Galveston. His office accepts MasterCard, Visa, HealthCap, and various insurance plans.

O.B. Jackson, Jr., M.D., F.A.C.S.
3509 Lawton • 451-0234

Lonn Bradley Lockhart, M.D.

Dr. Lockhart's practice is limited to pediatric ophthalmology and strabismus. He cares for the eyes of newborns through 18 years and includes a full range of services—diagnosis, treatment of medical and surgical problems, including strabismus (crossed eyes), cataracts, glaucoma, and more common vision problems, and prescriptions for glasses and contact lenses.

A graduate of the University of Texas Medical Branch in Galveston, Dr. Lockhart served his internship in Internal Medicine and his residency in Ophthalmology. He received a fellowship in Pediatric Ophthalmology at Children's Hospital of Pittsburgh and opened his practice in Austin in 1985. His examinations are extremely thorough, and he makes every effort to help the parent and child understand the procedures and results.

The visits are a pleasant and fun experience for the child. Eye tests, examination equipment, and the office itself are all designed to allow the child to relax, cooperate, and enjoy the experience. Dr. Lockhart has staff privileges at Brackenridge Children's Hospital, Seton, and St. David's. His office accepts MasterCard, Visa, Health Cap, and various insurance plans and HMOs.

Lonn Bradley Lockhart, M.D.
1305 West 34th St., Suite 410 • 458-1922
Open Monday, 11-7, Tuesday — Friday, 9-5

J.R. Rogers, O.D. and Garth Weaver, O.D.

Dr. Rogers is a graduate of the University of Houston College of Optometry and has been practicing at the Round Rock T.S.O. since 1981. Dr. Weaver is also a U.H.C.O. graduate and has been practicing in the Austin area since 1984. The T.S.O. in Round Rock provides family optometry with special emphasis on school-age children, contact lenses, geriatrics, and computer related vision problems. Patients are treated with patience and respect by doctors who are also trusted friends and members of the community. Every patient receives a thorough and careful examination, including tests of ocular health. They specialize in the prescription of contact lenses for adolescents and extended-wear lenses for adults. Corneal rehabilitation is another speciality of the clinic. Appointments are not necessary but are preferred. Saturdays are on a walk-in basis. MasterCard and Visa are accepted.

T.S.O. of Round Rock • J.R. Rogers, O.D. • Garth Weaver, O.D.
1202 N. IH 35 • Round Rock West Shopping Center • 255-7869

by Rachael Koeninger, age 7, Lake Austin Montessori

Gail T. Kendrick, Ph.D.

Dr. Kendrick is a psychologist (with health service provider status) in private practice here in Austin, Texas. A graduate of the Counseling Psychology Program at The University of Texas, Dr. Kendrick spent a predoctoral internship year in clinical psychology at The Children's Hospital Medical Center (Harvard Medical School) in Boston, Mass. There she specialized in the evaluation and treatment of children, adolescents, and their families. Dr. Kendrick completed her undergraduate degree at Wellesley College, Wellesley, Mass. and holds a master's degree in teaching from Harvard University. After completing a year of postdoctoral training in clinical psychology at Austin State Hospital (ASH), Dr. Kendrick was employed as a staff psychologist at the Children's Psychiatric Unit at ASH. Currently, besides her private practice, Dr. Kendrick is also affiliated with CPC Capital Hospital where she specializes in play therapy.

Gail T. Kendrick, Ph.D. • 7200 North MoPac Expwy., Suite 150-160 • 345-3266
Hours by appointment both days and evenings

Louisa R. Powell, Ph.D.

Dr. Powell consults with families, tests children, and provides therapy to people of all ages. Her specialties include working with preschoolers and helping to identify children with learning disabilities and children who are especially gifted. She makes recommendations for education and other activities so that they may achieve their maximum potential. She is willing to act as an advocate for the child with school administration or within the court system. Dr. Powell received her Ph.D. from the University of Chicago in 1973 and did her internship at the V.A. Hospital in Connecticut. She has consulted with schools and worked at Austin Child Guidance Center. She opened her private practice in 1981. She sees her practice as similar to that of the "family doctor" in that she works with the whole family. She enjoys working with parenting issues. She is a Preferred Provider for several insurance companies. Dr. Powell is available by appointment.

Louisa R. Powell, Ph.D.
4131 Spicewood Springs Road, Bldg. C-3 • 343-0118

"We give thanks for the gift of life, as we dedicate ourselves to the tenderness of understanding, the fairness of good care, and the intelligence of warm devotion."
—Robert Zoerheide

SUSAN L. McMILLAN, Ph.D. — PEDIATRIC PSYCHOLOGIST
3724 Jefferson, Suite 221 • 453-2935
Specializing in children & adolescents • Developmental problems
Parenting issues • Stress • School difficulties • Academic tutoring

ALL SAINTS EPISCOPAL DAY SCHOOL
209 West 27th Street • 472-8866
Age 3 through Pre-K; 8:45 am - 11:45 am & extended care; Kindergarten 8:45 am-2 pm
Balanced program of academic, physical and social experiences

BETHANY PRESCHOOL & MOTHER'S DAY OUT
10010 Anderson Mill Rd. • 258-6965
Preschool (2 1/2 - 4 years) • Mother's Day Out (11 mo. - 4 yrs.)
Specially designed facility. Highly qualified Christian staff.

PHOENIX SCHOOL
1207 West 9th St. • 474-1667
Unique blend of Montessori & unstructured activities
Infants - age 5 • 7:30 am - 5:45 pm

SACRED HEART CATHOLIC SCHOOL
5911 Reicher Drive • 926-0687
Program for 4 year olds that integrates academics with Christian
values • Open 7 am - 5:30 pm, School day: 7:55 am - 3 pm

ST. MARTIN'S LUTHERAN DAY SCHOOL
606 W. 15th St • 476-4037
P.E. • Music • Library • Computer • Spanish
Age 2 thru Third Grade • 7:15-5:45 • State adopted curriculum

THE WESLEY SCHOOL
6100 Berkman • 452-5796
Ages 2 1/2 - 1st grade • Part Time & Full Time • 7:15-5:45
Qualified staff in a nurturing Christian environment

TRINITY LUTHERAN SCHOOL & CHILD DEVELOPMENT CENTER
1207 West 45th Street • 453-0702
Ages 18 months through K • 7 am - 6 pm
Christ-centered education for your child

TRINITY PRESBYTERIAN CHILD DEVELOPMENT CENTER
5801 Westminster Drive • 928-2212
Open Monday - Friday, 7:15-5:30 • Ages 2-5
Children learn with love in small classes guided by skilled teachers

━━━━━━━━━━━━ ᨀ Montessori Schools ᨀ ━━━━━━

Austin Montessori School

Austin Montessori School puts into practice the visionary philosophy of Dr. Maria Montessori that is based on the principle that each child is an individual with unique needs, interests, and patterns of growth, and that given a maximum of spontaneity in choice of developmentally appropriate physical and intellectual activity, each will flourish in his own way.

The school, founded in 1967 by Donna Bryant Goertz, is the only one in Austin offering the continuity of Montessori education from two and one-half through twelve years of age. There are three beautiful campuses, one north and two south. The elementary campus has three spacious, well-equipped classrooms, a library, a music building, and a large playground. All of our teachers (guides) are A.M.I. certified. Preschool classes from 8:30—12 or 2:30; elementary classes from 8:30—3. Early arrival from 7:30 and after-school care until 5:30 are available.

Austin Montessori School
Three convenient campuses • Call 892-0253 for further information

Lake Austin Montessori

Lake Austin Montessori provides a flexible blend of Montessori philosophy, methodology, and materials with other instructional methods and materials selected to meet individual learning needs. Penny Koeninger became the owner of the school in 1984. Her goal was to meet the need in Austin for a school and extended-care program by providing an enriched environment for children and full-time quality child care for working parents. The goal of Lake Austin Montessori is to help each child feel good about himself, others, and learning. Practical life, language, math, reading, gymnastics, science, art, and music are taught by trained staff. The school also takes advantage of the Austin Nature Center, dance classes, swimming lessons, children theater productions, and others. Lake Austin Montessori provides ample opportunity for the parents to become involved with special seminars, newsletters, and volunteer programs.

Lake Austin Montessori • 715 Hearn • 477-7753
Open 7:15 am to 5:45 pm, Monday - Friday

ATHENA MONTESSORI SCHOOL, Inc.
2000 RALEIGH • 474-5507

Founded in 1967 by A.M.I. teacher Leo Nitch. Now directed by daughter, Holly Nitch Reed. Weekday mornings for ages two to six.

The Montessori Center
4108 Avenue H • Austin, TX 78751 • 451-5081
Open 7:30 am - 6 pm, Monday - Friday
For ages 2 - 6 • Affiliated with A.M.S.

by Brett Robertson, age 9, Toddle Inn

CHAPTER IV

Early School Years

(6-12 years)

by Raquel Gutierrez, Grade 1, Sanchez Elementary School

Alternatives in Education: Public and Non-Public Schools

by Lucy C. Nazro

"What kind of education do I want for my child?" This is perhaps the fundamental question that parents ask themselves. It is not, however, an easy question to answer, for there is a smorgasbord of educational opportunities available. In most parts of the country there are public schools, parochial schools, Montessori schools, schools for the learning impaired, schools for gifted and talented youngsters, independent unaffiliated schools, and independent church-related schools. Determining which option best suits a particular child requires hard thinking, careful investigation, and a clear understanding of what you really want for your children.

The education of a child is, after all, the primary responsibility which society places upon parents. It is a process which begins for the child at birth and continues long after the child matures. Education lasts throughout the life of every individual. The nurturing which parents offer their newborns is the first step in this process. The basic parental tasks of feeding, changing, loving, and caring for newborns are themselves experiences which teach trust, enable love, and establish basic values. Even in this day when very often both parents work and infant day care is a fact of life, the family remains the primary vehicle for teaching children values and giving them tools for making moral decisions and developing interpersonal relationships.

As the child grows, however, certain aspects of the learning process will necessarily take place outside the home. Children need the company of other children and adults outside the family to develop social skills, to test the values they are learning at home, and to explore new avenues of experience.

Certainly the great majority of parents answer this question by choosing public schools for their children. American public education has a long and distinguished history of enabling an educated citizenry to participate in the life of our nation. Public schools are schools for everyone—for bookworms and for athletes, for slow learners and for the gifted, for future professional men and women, and for those who want to learn a trade. Ideally public schools reflect the enormous richness and diversity of contemporary American society. Their stated values are the values of our American democracy with its vision of every individual's inalienable right to life, liberty, and the pursuit of happiness. Public school systems work hard at responding to new needs and new demands as American society changes, develops, and accepts new understandings of itself. They do this to come closer to meeting their all-embracing and all-encompassing goal of providing, within a single school or school system, a variety of learning experiences which answer the manifold needs of a pluralistic culture.

But Americans are a people who thrive on freedom of choice. We understand that a variety of options is not just desirable but absolutely necessary for our well-being. This is perhaps the basic justification for the existence of non-public schools. Such schools do not exist to supplant public education, but to enrich and augment the possibilities available in this all-important area of life.

The option is not simply public or private, for both sectors represent an often bewildering number of alternatives. Public schools, for example, offer a variety of programs and approaches based on student ability. Science, Fine Arts, and Humanities academies offer specialized learning experiences. So too, parochial and other church-related schools, for example, seek to foster and to further particular religious values which children learn at home. Some private schools place an enormous premium on the values of individual achievement within a competitive environment. Others seek to develop children within a caring community. College preparatory schools narrow the educational base by concentrating on the classic, humanistic academic disciplines—and even here there may be very real differences of approach from school to school. There are non-public schools which seek to limit diversity in the student population, while others bend over backwards to ensure just such diversity. There are no hard and fast rules which characterize the educational opportunities available in either public or non-public schools.

There are, on the other hand, a few generalizations that can be made. Public school systems in urban areas are large; decisions affecting the school population are made on the basis of thousands of students, parents, and teachers. Non-public schools are generally smaller and are, therefore, often able to make necessary changes with more concern for the particular needs of individuals. Public schools are free. Private schools depend on tuition, although scholarships are generally available for qualified students with demonstrable need. Public systems must redraw school boundary lines as neighborhood demographics and educational philosophies change. Private schools which draw from entire urban areas can be much more stable in this regard.

It was nearly 20 years ago that my husband and I had to answer the question about what sort of education we wanted for our children. Although we were ourselves both products of public education, when we had given the matter the very serious consideration it warranted, we opted for an independent church-related school. Our reasons were varied. We both wanted religion to be an important part of our children's lives—not just as a Sunday exercise, not as an academic discipline, but as an integral part of their education. We liked the caring and nurturing which was so much a part of that school's approach. We appreciated the benefits of small classes where individual attention was given.

Through the years we have moved several times and our children have been students in a number of schools. With only a couple of exceptions they have all been church-related. We are happy with the choices we made as we have seen our children grow and learn. We have seen values that we believe to be important become integral in their lives as well.

Certainly the answer we gave to the question of what kind of school was right for our children will not be everyone's answer. Nor should it be. There is no one answer to the question, no one right decision that can be made between public and non-public schools. To recognize how vital the question is and to answer it knowledgeably for one's own children is the important thing.

Lucy C. Nazro is Director of St. Andrew's Episcopal School.

Safe Sports

by Spanky Stephens

From the instant children are born, they are completely dependent on their parents for all worldly needs. Aside from the basic needs, parents have a never-ending job of providing the best they can afford for their child.

Once your child has reached the age to begin participating in a sports program, regardless of the type of sport it is, you should review the credentials of those persons providing your child with instruction. It would not be sensible to enter your child into a program that does not have qualified people to teach these programs.

As an athletic trainer, I am often asked by parents what factors to consider prior to enrolling a child in a sports program. My answer has always been that you should prepare a complete list of your questions about the program much as you would before going to a job interview. Based on the answers you receive, you can make a more educated decision about whether to enroll your child in this program. Here are some typical questions:

What qualifies this clinic, group, or individual to offer this sport to the public?

Almost everyone that teaches some type of sports activity must go through a certification process to teach it to the public. This certification should be displayed; if it is not, ask for proof of certification. If certification is not available, then you know that the group about which you are inquiring is not for your child. Most coaches and teachers today are required to have training in teaching a sport, as well as first aid and CPR training. These measures ensure that your child will be well taken care of both in training and in case of emergency.

How often is the equipment used by your child inspected by qualified people?

Each clinic has equipment that must be inspected periodically so that they know the equipment is safe for use. This equipment must meet certain standards for it to continue to be usable. If the equipment does not meet these standards, it cannot be used due to chance of injury.

Even those of you who wish to enter your child into youth football or soccer should be aware that the protective equipment worn by the participants must meet certain criteria for those sports. When purchasing this equipment at a sporting goods store, make certain that all your purchases meet the specific criteria for the sport in which your child will be involved.

What should I feed my child during these activities?

Studies have shown that the nutrition and the eating habits of your child at an early age have a lasting effect on eating habits later in life. Take time to read labels on all food that you buy; know exactly what you are feeding your child at all times.

Never feed your child a large meal closer than two hours before an activity. If you do, the child will be sluggish during the activity and have an increased chance of suffering from gastric upset. It takes about four hours for the stomach to empty. When a child is involved in an activity, the body all but closes down the normal absorption rate of food so that the blood can carry oxygen and energy to the muscles where it is needed for the activity. Thus, only 7 percent of energy-producing carbohydrates is absorbed during activity.

If your child is involved in a lengthy all-day or half-day session, give him or her healthy snacks, such as bagels, nutritional food bars, and fresh fruit, and plenty of fluid to take at breaks. All these are necessary for your child to maintain energy levels. These snacks are readily absorbed by the body.

Nutrition is important to the healthy lifestyle of your child. There are many courses available to the public through hospitals, nutritionists, and articles in various publications. Take time to learn about nutrition for your own healthy lifestyle and that of your family.

Safe sports

Safety in sports comes from you as a parent learning about the many aspects of sports. Asking questions is only the first step toward ensuring safety in the activities of your child. Remember, this *is* your child we are talking about; it is important to be informed and to keep your child informed.

Just because one family has its child in a particular sport does not make that sport the right one for your child. Look around and select an activity that is safe, as well as to your liking and to your child's liking.

Spanky Stephens is Head Athletic Trainer at the University of Texas at Austin.

by Andrew King, age 4, Phoenix School

Introducing Your Child to Pets

by Susan D. Eakle, DVM

Your children have been pleading and pestering for months or even years about wanting a pet. They promise to take care of it "no matter what." They may have already decided on what kind of animal they want. Finally you relent and agree that they are old enough to enjoy a pet and to help with the responsibility of caring for one.

Now a most important step begins, that of choosing the right pet for the child and the family. Often families are lucky and get an animal they love for many years. However, there are too many times when an animal is chosen that later becomes unmanageable or unacceptable because of its size, care needed, aggression, destructiveness or because the children lose interest or are overwhelmed by the pet. It is helpful to involve the child in the process of choosing a pet from the beginning. Knowing if any family member has allergies to any animals before bringing home a pet can avoid heartache later. Family discussions of the following questions may help guide you to your final choice of a new family member.

How much room do you have for a pet? Large and medium-size dogs require a fenced yard and need regular exercise. All dogs, especially small dogs, may be indoors a great deal but still need a controlled area for exercise and to use the bathroom. Cats may live entirely indoors. If they are going to be outdoors at all, it is almost impossible to confine them so the risks of busy streets and other cats or dogs attacking them need to be considered. Some other pets, like ferrets and rabbits, may be kept in cages or hutches outside under proper conditions or may be indoor pets. Smaller animals like hamsters, guinea pigs, snakes, and mice require even less room and less constant care. Birds and fish, on the other hand, often do not require much room but feeding and cleaning can be time consuming.

What place in the family will the pet occupy? Will it be one that is like a family member who goes on vacations, stays in the house, and sleeps with the child? Do the children want pets that will actively play with them? Dogs usually travel better than other animals. Medium- or large-size dogs do better with rough play, and small dogs may become snappy because they are frightened of being hurt. Certain breeds, like Labrador or Golden retrievers and some spaniels, usually are very good with children and will be patient with rough play. There are many dogs of other breeds and mixed breeds that can be wonderful pets as well, and every dog's personality needs to be considered separately.

Cats play in a different way. They may play more with toys or mock stalk and attack games rather than tolerating much rough handling. Some cats allow themselves to be handled for long periods and may even allow a small child to carry them around like dolls for hours. Again, every individual cat is different, although there are some breeds like Burmese or Ragdolls that are especially affectionate or calm. If you are interested in knowing the special temperaments of certain breeds, go to cat or dog shows where owners will often share information. Also there are books available in the library, and pet stores and veterinarians may be helpful.

While it might be surprising, there are many families who have very different pets. Many children love their pet ferrets, rats, hamsters, rabbits, and guinea pigs. At times these smaller pets are more a child's own special pet than the family dog or cat. Ferrets and rabbits need more space and care than the smaller animals. It might be best to talk to someone who has one of these pets if you are thinking of getting one. Sometimes teachers keep these animals in classrooms and will be able to tell you about them. Also veterinarians who treat these small pets can help.

How do you decide which individual animal is the right one? In almost all species of animals, those that are adopted at six to sixteen weeks of age will have more time to "socialize" to your family. This is an important time between weaning and four months of age when they are learning to accept different people and animals and are more adaptable to change. Try to look at puppies and kittens that are from homes where they are handled gently by people their entire lives. Choose an animal that is friendly and will come up to you. For puppies, roll them on their backs and see if they will allow themselves to be petted in this position for about 30 seconds. This means the puppy is willing to be submissive and will be easier to train. Watch the puppy play with its littermates. If it is always withdrawn or reluctant to play, it may be more timid and will require more patience, gentleness, and time to train. If it is terrorizing all the other puppies constantly and chews and aggressively climbs all over your child, it may be a more dominant dog and will require a more experienced and firmer hand to train. A dog between the two extremes will usually be a better choice.

Have your child hold the kitten in his arms and see how it responds to being held. A kitten that always struggles and doesn't want to be held may be less affectionate and tolerant of handling. A kitten that bites hard or plays roughly all the time may be too aggressive for a child. Older puppies and kittens and adult animals can be tested the same way. When you choose your pet, request that you be allowed to take the new animal to a veterinarian to be sure it is healthy before the adoption is final. Try to take the child on this and subsequent visits to the pet's doctor to help the child understand and be involved in the pet's care.

Make preparations for your new pet before you bring it home. Involve the child in each step of this preparation. Buy food and water bowls, food, a toy or two, and even a bed or scratching post. There are books that will take you through the steps of owning a new pet, and reading these aloud to a child may be helpful. Some responsibilities that may be discussed before the pet comes home might include feeding, watering, exercising a dog, keeping gates or doors closed, keeping toys and string picked up, and rules about bathroom training. Doing this before the pet comes home may enhance the sense of responsibility, and also the pet will be less confused and will respond better.

Most pets live for many years, often much of a child's childhood, so taking time to choose the right pet will benefit your family for many years. Preparing ahead of time for the homecoming and having the child actively participate in choosing a pet helps in the adjustment period. Now it is time to sit back and enjoy watching a child and his pet play and share the love that they can bring to each other.

Susan Eakle is a veterinarian.

Childhood Orthodontics

by Albert H. Owen III, D.D.S., M.S.D.

No one wants to have crooked teeth or a funny-looking smile, even young children. Whereas traditionally, orthodontic treatment was started during the teenage years, today there are many orthodontists who start treatment much earlier. Early orthodontic treatment may be started as early as age seven, but sometimes even earlier if the parents, family dentist, pediatric dentist, or other health-care provider notices a problem. Early orthodontic treatment has the advantages of being able to influence the direction the jaws are growing, and younger teeth, jaws, and muscles are easier to move.

Some of the specific problems that early treatment can correct include:

- Crowding—where the jaws are too small for all the teeth
- Overbites—where the top teeth stick out over the bottom teeth
- Underbites—where the bottom teeth come out in front of the top teeth
- Crossbites—where the back teeth are crossed over backwards
- Habits—finger or thumb sucking, poor swallowing or mouth breathing
- Jaw Joint problems—where the joints don't work well due to the bad bite

Each of these problems can cause major imbalances in your child's growing mouth. When these problems are left alone until the teenage years, the correction is harder, takes longer, and may be more costly.

Early treatment usually requires a thorough diagnosis to be sure of the extent of the problem. There are many different types of problems, and each one is unique. Individualized treatment is the key to getting the best results. After the diagnosis and treatment plan have been carefully thought out, then your child may receive one of the following appliances:

- Palatal Expander—which widens an upper jaw that is too narrow
- Habit Corrector—which helps discourage thumbsucking, finger sucking, poor swallowing, or mouth breathing
- Functional Appliance—which helps guide the jaws as they grow into a more balanced bite
- Headgear—which helps correct buck teeth
- Retainers—which are used for thousands of individual tooth problems
- Braces—limited braces at this time may be necessary to correct local tooth problems

The average treatment time varies tremendously according to the actual problem, patient cooperation, and the appliance used, but you can expect early orthodontic treatment to last between 15 and 30 months.

Everyone knows braces can straighten crooked teeth and create a beautiful smile. In addition to a beautiful smile, the scope of early orthodontic treatment includes the basic goal of creating a healthier environment in which teeth can grow. Better bites mean straighter teeth, and straighter teeth can provide the following benefits:

Straight teeth are easier to keep clean.

Straight teeth will have fewer problems with gum disease.

Straight teeth chew better, and this improves digestion.

Straight teeth are in better balance with the jaw joints, keeping them healthy.

Straight teeth obviously look better, and this helps improve self-esteem.

The value of self-esteem cannot be over-estimated. As our children grow up to take their places as productive members of society, the value of their self-confidence is priceless. A child's self-esteem is fragile and we, as adults, must do everything we can to encourage a strong and positive self-image. The pictures below show a child at age five with an obvious imbalance in her facial profile. There was genuine concern for her chewing problems, but her poor self-image was of major concern even at this young age. After about two years of early orthodontic treatment, the same child has a new profile, a greatly improved bite, and an equally improved self-image. Who knows the long-term consequence for this child if her poor bite, poor jaw balance, and poor self-esteem had been left untreated for several more years?

Before orthodontic treatment   *After orthodontic treatment*

You may be wondering if early orthodontic treatment can prevent treatment later. Realistically, early treatment does not prevent braces altogether, but it does significantly reduce the time needed for braces. This is because most of the original problems have been reduced or corrected. Since the braces treatment is shorter, usually the fee will be less as well. Probably the overall fee for early and regular orthodontic treatment will be slightly more than for braces alone, but the results will be commensurately better. Most often, early orthodontic treatment will be able to avoid pulling permanent teeth to correct the crowding or overbite. Not pulling permanent teeth has the potential advantages of having a stronger bite, a fuller and more attractive smile, and more natural treatment. However, non-extraction treatment usually requires more effort on the part of the patient because in extraction treatment much of the work is done by the extractions themselves.

In summary, the overall concept of early orthodontic treatment is that pre-ventive medicine is better than corrective medicine. Another way of saying it is, "An ounce of prevention is worth a pound of cure."

Albert H. Owen III is a board-certified orthodontist.

Does Your Child Have Emotional Problems?
by Nelson Ceballos, M.D.

The first clue that your child might need outside help is a general change in his or her normal behavior that lasts more than a few weeks. Your child may express to you feelings of:
1. Sadness, unhappiness, hopelessness, or worthlessness
2. Anger, fear, excessive worry, death wishes
3. Physical illnesses or complaints, such as stomach aches, nausea, headaches, sleeplessness, and lump in throat
4. Believing that he or she is fat when actually thin

Many times adolescents and children have difficulty putting their feelings into words, but their actions can tell you many things if you pay attention. Some of the actions that you may see when your child needs help with emotional problems are:
1. Refusal to attend school
2. Withdrawal and isolation from family and friends
3. Inability to relax and enjoy normal activities
4. Inability to concentrate, easily frustrated over school work
5. Excessive lies, truancy, running away
6. Frequent changes in mood characterized by severe depression followed by feelings of high energy and high mood and spirits
7. Repetitive actions, such as excessive washing of hands or constantly putting things in order
8. Dramatic fluctuation in weight
9. Eating excessively and then going to the bathroom
10. Excessive sadness over the loss of friends, romantic relations, or family members.

Preventing problems
I'm sure you have heard the saying that the time to prevent a crisis is before it happens. Getting to know yourself and your child should be a priority for you. Take time in your busy day to talk with and listen to your child. The better you know him or her, the easier it will be to tell when behavior changes.

It is important to remember that your child is not a small adult, but a child who counts on you to serve as a role model and provider. Many of us as parents benefit from parenting classes being taught in our own community. Join parent support groups, participate in school activities, learn all you can about problems facing our youth and community. Remember, you serve as a mirror for your child, and the reflection he or she sees is the one he or she reflects.

Drugs and alcohol
How can you tell if your children are using drugs or alcohol? Again, your first clue is a change in their normal behavior. School failure or changes in dress, sleep, eating, and friends are sometimes the most obvious changes in behavior. Your child may have physical symptoms, such as swollen or red eyes, tremors of the hand, dilated pupils, and uncontrollable outbursts of anger. Your children are at a higher risk for drug and alcohol abuse if drug addition and alcoholism has affected another member of your family. It is also important to note what kind of

friends your child hangs around with. Observe them and take note of their behavior. Especially for adolescents, the need to conform with their peers is great.

Medication in treatment

In many cases emotional problems in children and adolescents cannot be solved with therapy alone due to the child's inability to control thoughts, feelings, and actions. Recent studies prove that the concurrent use of medication and therapy can enhance and accelerate recovery. It is important to understand that emotional problems can be as life threatening as physical illness.

There are many medications used in the treatment of children and adolescents. It is important for you the parents to ask questions about the use of medication and to become knowledgeable about them. Do not be afraid to ask questions of your physician.

Suicide

There are ways of knowing when your child or adolescent is at risk of suicide. There may be a manifestation of depression, anxiety, aggression against self, preoccupation with self, disappointment with the parents, failure in academic performance, sports, friendship, and the dissolution of romantic relationships. There is a history of isolation, decrease in human contact or expectations by self and the parents, alcohol and drug abuse, parental disharmony, and conflict with the parents among children who attempt suicide. Identification with the suicidal behavior of a friend, a relative, or a national figure may also precipitate the suicidal behavior. The giving away of prized objects may indicate a suicidal preoccupation. Verbalization of suicide or death wishes, such as "I wish I was not around" or "Soon I'll be out of your way" should be taken seriously. Failure in human contact is the most significant contributing factor to the development of depression in children and adolescents.

Adolescence is a stressful time, and suicidal acts may be a reaction to the long-term stress experienced by many adolescents or to a particular stressful situation. Those adolescents with poor control or those who are hypersensitive are more likely to fall into the category of suicide attempters.

Depression is the most common characteristic present in suicidal adolescents, but this may not present itself as clinical depression but may appear masked as boredom, restlessness, or delinquent behavior. Depressed and suicidal adolescents and children usually have low self-esteem. They usually experience loneliness, hopelessness, and worthlessness. Behavior and character disorders are common in suicidal adolescents, as are aggression, impulsiveness, and poor judgment. Many suicidal adolescents may appear withdrawn, particularly from their parents. The most frequent precipitating event is a "disciplinary crisis."

The following are characteristics of suicidal children and adolescents: disphoric mood (feeling sad, depressed, despondent, hopeless, irritable), loss of energy and fatigue, low self-esteem, poor school performance, anhedonia (inability to experience pleasure), change in appetite, insomnia, sleep problems, suicidal ideations (thoughts of death or thoughts and feelings of suicide), loss of interest in social activities, and/or feelings of worthlessness or guilt.

Dr. Nelson Ceballos is Board Certified in Child and Adolescent Psychiatry.

Austin Montessori School

Austin Montessori School puts into practice the visionary philosophy of Dr. Maria Montessori that is based on the principle that each child is an individual with unique needs, interests, and patterns of growth, and that given a maximum of spontaneity in choice of physical and mental activity will flourish.

The school, founded in 1967 by Donna Bryant Goertz, is the only one in Austin offering the continuity of Montessori education from two and one-half through twelve years of age. Each of our classrooms offers a rich and ordered environment which has been specially prepared for the children and which offers a wide variety of attractive materials designed to lead them naturally and logically from concrete experiences to abstract ideas. Major areas of development include practical life, language, mathematics, geography, history, science, and the arts.

There are three beautiful primary campuses, one north and two south. The elementary campus has three spacious, well-equipped classrooms, a library, music building, large playing fields, and a playground. In addition to primary and elementary classes, we offer after-school enrichment programs, early arrival, music lessons, and a shuttle bus. All of our teachers (guides) are A.M.I. certified. Preschool classes are from 8:30 until 12 or 2:30, and elementary classes are from 8:30 until 3. Early arrival from 7:30 and after-school care until 5:30 are available.

Austin Montessori School
Three convenient campuses • Call 892-0253 for further information

Kirby Hall School

Kirby Hall's goal is to be a strong Christian college-preparatory school which educates able students well and instills a feeling of self-worth and a strong sense of ethics. Education offered in a loving and caring manner encourages the development of well-rounded and competent students who will become generous and positive members of their community. Each individual is accepted and appreciated for his or her uniqueness. Parents and students choose Kirby Hall for excellent teaching, a well-rounded school life, and individual attention for each student.

Organized in 1976, the school serves children from kindergarten through 12th grade. The average performance of students is well above the national norm, and all graduating seniors score above the nation's average for college-bound seniors on nationally scored tests. The curriculum stresses English, math, science, languages, and history, plus physical education and fine arts. Extracurricular fun includes trips, lectures, banquets, dances, sports, performances, and holiday celebrations. Kirby Hall welcomes students who have demonstrated a strong motivation to learn and an ability to work harmoniously with others.

Kirby Hall School
306 West 29th • 474-1770 or 474-1771

St. Theresa's School

This popular West Austin school is located near Cat Mountain (off R.R. 2222) between MoPac and The Capital of Texas Highway. St. Theresa's School was founded in 1985 and has enjoyed a steady increase in enrollment and grade levels. The school offers limited enrollment in Pre-K through grade 4. Growth plans include adding a new grade yearly until this school reaches grade levels Pre-K through 6. The school is the fastest growing member of the Austin Catholic Diocese School System.

In addition to addressing the state-required basic skills, St. Theresa's School offers an exemplary curriculum, which provides enrichment in all academic areas. Programs are provided in fine arts, Spanish, and computer-based instruction. A special feature of the school is an on-campus zoo.

The staff of St. Theresa's School believe that each child is a gift from God. The school goal is to assist each student in realizing his/her full potential through spiritual, intellectual, social, moral, and physical development. After-school child care is provided on campus by the Stepping Stone Child Development Center.

Formal pre-registration occurs in early February. The school is usually full with a waiting list. Call for more information.

St. Theresa's School
4310 Small Drive • 451-7105

by Meredith Littlepage, age 7, Oak Hill Day Care

The Isely School

Originally started in 1957 by Ruth Isely, The Isely School is now owned and operated by Eva Foerster and Mary Brown, experienced master teachers who use innovative techniques to help motivate and inspire students. The school advances a unique "child-centered" philosophy that fosters social, intellectual, emotional, and physical growth. Not limited to a single learning approach, the school makes use of many child development and learning theories. A real love and concern for children, plus years of successful teaching, enable faculty at The Isely School to meet the specific needs of each child. The school offers individualized instruction in language arts, math, science, social studies, history, geography, art, music, Spanish, and physical education. The school believes that a strong academic future is built on a foundation of learning skills—self-organization, self-motivation, problem solving, creative thinking, and independence. Kindergarten through third grade.

The Isely School • 2301 Shoal Creek Blvd. • 478-1277

Sacred Heart Catholic School

Established in 1963, Sacred Heart School offers a complete education with high academic and spiritual standards for students in pre-kindergarten through sixth grade. Programs focus on spiritual, academic, emotional, and social dimensions of life. Teacher preparation, adult assistants, and praise and encouragement of students foster a quiet learning environment. Emphasis on Catholic values, small group instruction, and up-to-date facilities and equipment provide the groundwork for excellence in basic education. The school augments basic education with many special programs and elective opportunities, including community service.

Sacred Heart Catholic School • 5911 Reicher Dr. • 926-0687
School day: 7:55 am - 3 pm Extended Day Care: 7 am - 5:30 pm

St. Andrew's School

Founded in 1952 by leaders from Good Shepherd, All Saints, and St. David's Episcopal churches, St. Andrew's was established specifically to provide an Episcopal elementary school for all of Austin. St. Andrew's today offers an elementary and middle school centrally located to serve all geographical areas of Austin. An enriched curriculum offers basic academic education, plus enrichment programs in the fine arts, physical education, and foreign language study from grades one through eight.   Daily chapel is the focal point of life at the school which stresses values for everyday living. High expectations are held for each student, and the large, long-tenured faculty gives a sense of continuity which creates a healthy and supportive learning environment.   Grades 1-4 attend school from 8 am until 3 pm. Grades 5-8 attend school from 8 am until 3:30 pm. After-school care from 3-5:30 pm offers enrichment classes and study hall.

St. Andrew's School
1112 West 31st St. • 452-5779

St. Martin's Lutheran Day School

The most important concern at St. Martin's is the welfare of the individual student. The primary goals are to provide quality educational opportunities to all children at all levels, and to develop the whole child mentally, emotionally, and spiritually through a stimulating program. St. Martin's offers a state-adopted curriculum, including Spanish, computer, P.E., music, and gymnastics. Library and Chapel are once a week. A Christian education is provided for children two years of age through the third grade. The school has a teaching staff with years of experience, reasonable tuition rates, and a loving and nurturing atmosphere. St. Martin's opened in 1962 and is accredited by the American Lutheran Education School. Small classes ensure that children get the individual attention and nurturing they need. A summer day camp is also available. Tuition may be paid monthly, bimonthly, or weekly. Discounts are offered for the second sibling.

St. Martin's Lutheran Day School • 606 West 15th • 476-4037
Open 7:15 am to 5:45 pm, Monday - Friday

HOPE LUTHERAN SCHOOL AND CHILD DEVELOPMENT CENTER
6414 North Hampton Dr. (near Hwy. 290 East & Berkman) • 926-8574
Two Year Olds — Sixth Grade • Small Classes
Quality Christian Education • Caring Certified Teachers

The Merit School
2023 Denton Drive at Metric Blvd. • 837-8840
Open 6:30-6:30, Pre-Kindergarten - 3rd Grade &
After-School Program • See Creative World Profile

"Many of us, as parents, live with children from day to day. In a real sense this is an awesome fact. The clay of us is the clay of them, and the spirit of us, the holy, the sound, becomes the spirit of them as they look to us directly and subtly for shaping and guidance. The clay is all shaped but the holy is still being born. Out of our deep need for guidance and inspiration we pray for beauty and tenderness, for strength and integrity, for courage to face life strong and true, for joy to seize the delight of life and make it ever ring with laughter in the memories which shape the future."
—William B. Rice

Central Texas Counseling & Family Therapy

Central Texas Counseling & Family Therapy provides mental health services for individuals, couples, families, and children of all ages. A diagnosis, evaluation, and treatment program designed with the aid of client consultation helps resolve a variety of kinds of problems. Kay Hibbs holds a master's degree in family therapy and counseling psychology. She is a Licensed Professional Counselor and a Clinical Member of the American Association of Marriage & Family Therapy. Her background includes clinical work in individual, marriage, and family therapy, as well as program development for adolescent day treatment.

An emphasis is placed on both individuals and the relationship dynamics. Trained in both individual and relational therapies, Kay Hibbs provides an individualized process that involves insight, choice, tools, and a learned problem solving style that lasts a lifetime. The office accepts MasterCard and Visa and will assist in filing insurance claims. Hours by appointment.

Central Texas Counseling & Family Therapy Center
13915 Burnet Road, Suite 205 • 244-7555
5100 Midway Dr., Temple • 817/773-0016

Kathy A. Sheley, Ph.D. Austin Family Center

Dr. Sheley looks at a child from a systems view; that is, she asks who are the important people in the child's life and tries to coordinate each person's efforts in the same direction at the same time to expedite treatment. Because of the wide variety of certification and training, Dr. Sheley can treat the whole family, either individually or together. She uses play therapy and parent-child observation, as well as individual and/or family therapy, to help assess and treat certain problems.

A Health Service Provider in psychology, Dr. Sheley opened her practice in Austin in 1980. She is an Approved Supervisor for the American Association for Marriage and Family Therapy and a Certified Sex Therapist. She did her residency at the University of Texas Medical Branch at Galveston and taught for two years at the U.T. Health Science Center in San Antonio. She received her Master's and Ph.D. in clinical psychology from the University of Florida. She currently supervises student therapist trainees from the University of Texas at Austin through the Capital Area Mental Health Center. Dr. Sheley's office is centrally located one block west of MoPac North. Clients seen by appointment only.

Kathy A. Sheley, Ph.D.
5926 Balcones Drive, Suite 215 • 453-6688

Kathleen Adams, Ph.D.

Dr. Adams specializes in long-term psychotherapy (nine months or longer), concentrating on uncovering the deepest layers of confusion, disappointment, and despair, and helping her patients heal from within so that they can be free to learn, work, and play—in short, to thrive. Her psychotherapy style is to create an atmosphere of intimacy and intensity and personal honesty. Dr. Adams works with ages six years and up and her specialty is pre-adolescent girls. She also works with adults. Her practicing "co-therapist" is a golden retriever who helps put children at ease. Her office is a relaxing place with a separate play area.

A graduate of Cornell University and UT-Austin with a specialization in children, Dr. Adams served seven years as Chief Psychologist at Austin State Hospital and was coordinator of children's services at Central County MH/MR.

Kathleen Adams, Ph.D. • 3355 Bee Caves Rd., Suite 611 • 327-8311
Hours by appointment

Virginia Wirtz Shepperd, M.Ed.

A Certified Social Worker and Advanced Clinical Practitioner, Virginia Shepperd offers counseling to people who are depressed, who want to improve their relationships and their lives, and who want insight into their behavior problems. She works with children and adolescents, and helps with parenting issues. The mother of eight, Virginia can empathize with her clients and tailors therapy to the needs and understanding of each client. Because of her eclectic background, she has many approaches to use. A graduate of U.T. Austin, she has continued her training by attending workshops in various fields. Her Austin office is open 10-8 on Tuesday, 9:30-11:30 on Wednesday, and 10-8 on Thursday. The Marble Falls office is open all day Monday and Friday and Wednesday afternoon.

Virginia Wirtz Shepperd, M.Ed., C.S.W., A.C.P., L.P.C., AAMFT
1011 W. 31st, Suite 507 • Austin • 452-8504
1819 Lacy Dr. • Marble Falls • 693-3430

CHARTER LANE HOSPITAL — CHILDREN'S DISCOVERY PROGRAM
8402 Cross Park Dr. • 837-1800, 1-800-472-7422
A comprehensive program exclusively designed for children 3-12 suffering from emotional problems, abuse, conduct or behavioral disorders. In-house school.

Texas Child Care, Inc. - Oak Hill Summer Camp
5710 McCarty Lane • Austin, TX 78749 • 892-2273
Sports • Water activities • Music • Dance • Gymnastics
Karate • Science • Skating • Campouts

Albert H. Owen, III, D.D.S., M.S.D. &
David L. Hime, D.D.S., M.S.

Dr. Owen is a board-certified orthodontist. He graduated from Baylor College of Dentistry in Dallas in 1969 with highest scholastic honors. He also received his graduate orthodontic training from Baylor. He established his practice in Austin in 1973. Dr. Owen has received the outstanding clinic award from the Southwestern Society of Orthodontists. He is the author of more than 25 articles published in orthodontic journals and four booklets on various orthodontic treatments, and lectures to various orthodontic groups across the country.

Dr. David L. Hime, D.D.S., joined Dr. Owen as an associate in 1988. He received his B.S. degree in Chemical Engineering from Texas A&M and his D.D.S. degree from the University of Texas Dental Branch in Houston. He received his M.S. in Oral Biology and Certificate in Orthodontics from the University of Louisville.

The clinic provides childhood, adolescent, and adult orthodontic care. An emphasis is placed on interceptive and preventative orthodontics. The doctors focus not only on the teeth, but also on the whole person, his attitude, personality, and lifestyle. The office accepts MasterCard, Visa, and American Express, and will work with clients on payment plans. They will also handle insurance claims.

Albert H. Owen, III, D.D.S., M.S.D. & David L. Hime, D.D.S., M.S.
3624 North Hills Dr. • 345-0311
Open Mon., Tues., Thurs., 7—7; Wed., 8—5, Fri., 8—12

by Camille Laby, age 10, Austin Montessori School

All God's Creatures

The clinic provides medical care for dogs, cats, birds, rodents, reptiles, rabbits—in short, any and all of God's creatures. Surgical care, dental care, radiology, and diagnostic laboratory aids are provided. Personalized, caring attention is given by Dr. Leo G. Staley and his friendly, supportive staff. Dr. Staley graduated from Kansas State University in 1966 and has a master's degree in public health in addition to his veterinary degree. He has been in practice in Austin since 1981 and emphasizes to parents the appropriate safeguards to protect children from pet-related illnesses. Dr. Staley emphasizes preventative health for pets and good nutrition. He encourages questions and devotes his time, patience, and sense of humor to answering each one. The clinic accepts MasterCard, Visa, and Health Cap. The doctor's hours are by appointment.

**All God's Creatures • 14611 Burnet Rd. • 244-2235
Open Monday - Friday, 7 am to 7 pm; Saturday, 9 to 3**

Animal Care Clinic

Complete medical and surgical care for all household pets is provided by Animal Care Clinic. These services include surgery, orthopedic care, radiology, geriatric care, vaccinations, neutering, dermatology, and pre- and post-natal care. Dental services for pets, including cleaning, cavities, and extractions, are available.

A pet supply store within the clinic also provides a full line of products for pets, including dietary products, grooming aids, insecticide supplies, leashes, collars, bowls, and carrying cases. Pet grooming is also available. The clinic accepts Visa, MasterCard, and VET card. Vet Card offers a payment plan.

**Animal Care Clinic
1401 S. IH-35 • 338-2222**
Clinic Open—Mon. - Fri., 6:30-6; Hospital—Sat., 8-12; Pet Supply—M-F, 8-4

SUSAN D. EAKLE, D.V.M.
**Veterinarian (Small animal medicine & surgery)
3407 Northland Dr. • 453-5828
Open: Monday - Friday, 7-6; Saturday, 8-12**

"*Let our children learn to be honest, both with themselves and with all others. This is the basic human value. In its simplest terms, it is the capacity to distinguish clearly between what is and what is not, and thus to deal effectually with reality.*

"*Let our children learn to love truth. No matter whence it comes, so it be truth let them freely accept it, even when it goes against them. If they do this, they will not be much hampered by prejudice, for wherever truth can enter, prejudice cannot long remain. Moreover, by fidelity to truth the mind is nourished and becomes well grown.*

"*Let our children find courage and discover that they are stronger than the things of which they are afraid. Courage in our dealings with our own lives, courage in speaking out for the right, in condemning injustice, in standing for good against evil, courage to remain loyal to a deep conviction at whatever cost.*

"*Let our children cultivate breadth of humanity: a cordial welcome not merely for the factional, the provincial, the sectarian when they are good, but for whatever is beneficial to the human race no matter whence it comes.*

"*Let our children cultivate kindness, for it does not often come without cultivation, and it is needed: the world is too harsh.*

"*Let our children cultivate humility. Let our children learn that they are like other people, even the people they tend to despise; and that there is good and bad in all of us, and that each of us must make a hard struggle to bring the good out on top. Then, because of their own lost battles, they will acquire a gentle wisdom and walk softly where other people might get hurt.*"

—A. Powell Davies

CHAPTER V

Adolescence

(12-17 years)

by Paul Hernandez, Grade 5, St. Elmo Elementary School

Parenting the Teenager

by John A. Boston, Jr., M.D., L.F.A.P.A.

Each family is separate and different from every other, as are the individuals within the family. This means that few rules or guidelines can fit all situations. On the other hand, American families have much in common and may share similar concerns over the rearing of teenage children.

The task for the adolescent is to let go of childhood, adjust to changes in himself, and finally to separate from his parents by being an adult. For the parents the challenge is to gradually let go while still furnishing support and guidance during the years 12 to 19.

The adolescent can be as much fun as a new baby! Just as the infant explores a fresh world, the adolescent gradually discovers the adult world. In doing this, he may become disillusioned with parents as he discovers their human qualities. He may argue about rules and learn things by doing so. In early adolescence he may choose to idealize a rock musician or some movie actor. Conflicts about teenage sex, masturbation, and guilt may make him want to give up religion. One common experience for the young teenager is to have vivid dreams in which his parents die.

Typical concerns about a daughter are her popularity, dating behavior, drinking, drugs, grades, and the allowance. Concerns about the son put less emphasis on popularity and dating. Conformity to family rules, car use, and grades are stressed. Society no longer only sees marriage for the girl and a career for the son as the only options. Today's adolescents are freer in many ways than were earlier generations.

Advice on parenting adolescents traditionally emphasizes communication and flexibility. In every situation, you are setting an example for your child, whether it involves telling the truth, the use of drugs and alcohol, or dealing with other people. You need to be honest in your dealings with the teenager and flexible enough to allow him or her to experiment with decision (and mistake) making. You also need to encourage those characteristics in the teenager. If you are dishonest with either the child or others, he will assume that this is acceptable behavior. Forcing confessions from a child will often encourage him to lie to avoid punishment. Dole out punishment based on evidence rather than forced confessions. Encouraging honesty in other ways is important too. A regular allowance gives the teenager some freedom and discourages his trying to get money in dishonest ways.

Sex is a subject of great interest to the adolescent. You need to provide information in as straight-forward a manner as possible, even though it may make you uncomfortable at times. Adolescents need to know the facts, but they do not need to know about the sexual behavior of their parents. Solid love and affection from parents and other adults help the adolescent to be conservative in his or her sexual behavior. The United States produces one quarter million illegitimate children per year, many born to adolescent girls. Western European countries have much fewer teenage pregnancies. If you want your adolescent to be sexually responsible, you have to provide honest information. Closing your eyes and hoping for the best simply doesn't work.

Divorce often complicates parenting the adolescent. It makes for greater dependence on the single parent, and yet there is less support for that parent. If the single mother tells the adolescent bad things about the father to justify the divorce, she alienates the child and makes a good identity more difficult to achieve. When sons and daughters have been away from fathers for a long time, there can be advantages in their living with the father, even if the mother disapproves of him or his lifestyle. Divorced parents must avoid the temptation to use adolescents as their battleground for old wars between them.

Early in the teenage years, children exercise their changing social judgments by spending hours on the telephone or by forming cliques or groups. If a girl is left out, she feels unpopular and depressed. Sometimes the remedy is for her to achieve a feeling of being popular with her own mother, to know that her mother likes her. The peer popularity problem may disappear at that point. It can be valuable for parents to do something special with each individual child. Both sons and daughters need time as individuals with both mothers and fathers. Father may be good about taking a son hunting, but never take a daughter to lunch. Make a special effort to find something you can do with each of your children—just the two of you. It will give you an opportunity to get to know the teenager better and give the teenager the support he or she needs at this shaky time in life.

Age 14 is often the low point in adolescence. Feelings of depression and self-destruction fantasies are common. If the parents can be close but not too close at that time—a matter of being available but not intrusive—the storms can be weathered. Age 16, by contrast, is often a very good year.

Teenage years are often difficult for both parent and child. Your 15-year-old son or daughter may stir up unpleasant memories of your own 15th year. Each step the teenager makes toward independence is frightening for both of you—the child because it is all new and scary, and you because you are facing letting go of your child. Honesty and gentleness, coupled with good humor, are good tools in getting through these times. The years of rearing teenagers should be an opportunity for self-examination for both parents and kids, flavored with optimism for the future.

Dr. John A. Boston, Jr. is a psychiatrist specializing in children and adolescent care in Austin.

by Buckley Milburn, age 4, Lake Austin Montessori

Teens: How to Communicate with Your Parents

by Michael J. Sliwa and Kay G. Hibbs

Parents (we know you are reading this), this is an invitation to you to think back a few years to the time when you were a teenager. This may be difficult. It is hard to go back in a process you have already been through, to experience needs, emotions, and beliefs you do not experience now. If, as teenager or parent, any of the following thoughts have a ring of familiarity, spend a few minutes together discussing this article. It could help you understand each other and the role communication may play in the process of change. There are reasons for optimism. Teenagers and parents can have constructive relationships once they begin to have mutual respect and communicate as adults. By communicating as adults, we mean showing understanding, empathy, trust, patience, kindness, and honesty.

First though, please make an observation. Teenager, your parents are human beings. Parents, your teenager is a human being. That all comes as a shock, but someone had to tell you. If you agree that parents and teenagers are human beings, you can accept that all are capable of doing great things and that—on occasion—all are capable of human error.

Now teenagers. . . . You are certain that your parents never listen to you, cannot/do not understand you, and do not even like you all that much. You are sure that they would die if they only knew you had. . . . At times you may be certain that you are so bad or so dumb that everything you do is terrible. You may feel you are not worth talking to. For weeks you may feel positive your parents are "deadheads," bent solely on making life unbearable. Let's begin with a single question: How did you get the way you are? When we begin to understand the answer to this question for ourselves and others, we create an atmosphere for healthy communication.

"Tina, we've always done everything for you."

When you were a baby, mother and father were totally responsible for your activities and most of your needs. When you were young, they made all your decisions for you, cooked your meals, clothed you, provided for your education, guarded your safety, maintained your health, and supervised your social engagements. Most parents feel their children are part of them. Many parents find it is difficult to know where they stop and you begin. That is why some parents think that what the child does or what the teenager does reflects on them.

"Eric, when you mess up, it is like I mess up."

There are times that we realize every human being is responsible for his or her own actions, but because we are human, we also forget. Parents can work at remembering. Teenagers can remind them once in a while. Your parents may not remember that teenagers are putting into action what they have learned for the past 12 years or so. The teenager has succeeded—at least to some degree— in learning about living. You have learned how to trust, how to take risk, how to make decisions, how to handle mistakes. You know when you succeed and when you fail.

"Mom, I was afraid you would laugh at me."

Although you are using these skills to function in life, you may forget to demonstrate them to your parents. Why? You fear Mom will laugh or Dad will ground you. This is because your development in these skills combined with your needs as a teenager are difficult for your parents to identify with. You may have a great need to develop yourself socially, while your parents may demand academic performance. Teenager, it is time to risk letting your parents know what you are up against in your life. Mom may laugh or Dad may explode, but once the dust settles, you may find they are willing to listen to how well you are managing. There can be true benefits ahead if you let them know how you handle being around drugs or alcohol, what you did in a certain situation, and how you feel, think, and believe. What will happen the first time you begin to communicate as an adult? It's almost impossible to predict.

"Dad is going to hit the ceiling."

Father may respond from his fears and continue to try to shield you. Mother may say you should not feel a certain way. Parents may begin to realize that you can protect yourself. They may be willing to let you come to your own conclusions, even if yours are not exactly the same as theirs.

"Jennifer, I don't want to see you in a hospital emergency room."

Teenager, you may have to explain several times to your parents that those are your problems, feelings, and beliefs you are up against—and that you would like their help and feedback about them. Unless you want them, you may have to gently remind your parents that you are not asking for protection, judgment, or sympathy. Once your parents know what your life is like, you may be able to draw from their experience, advice, and knowledge. They will have an easier time seeing that you are trying to make the best decisions you can—for you. But you also must be sensitive to their fears. Reassure them.

"Dad, if the party gets out of hand, I will walk away."

What parents fear most is losing their children. And, if you are honest, what teenagers fear most is loss of their parents. As you take responsibility and make your own decisions, you probably will make some mistakes. It will be difficult for parents to watch that happen. They may get angry. They may punish. Stay with it; risk and decision-making will be two of your most valuable tools in the adult world. You already know what Mom or Dad is likely to do in a given situation. You may lose some privileges—so from the start that loss needs to be a part of your assessment of the risk ahead. Teenager, if you truly are ready to have a constructive relationship with your parents, let them know you are willing to suffer the consequences of your actions. Discuss mistakes with them. They can supply information that will help you avoid future errors. Teenagers, let your parents know that you need home to be a safe place, that you need a place where you can feel free to talk about your life, a place where you can gain constructive input. Tell them you need a place where you can be afraid of the world, a place to which you can retreat as you decide how to cope with life.

Communicate that home needs to be a place to be when you get angry, when you have hurts to be healed, when you need to be loved.

Michael Sliwa and Kay Hibbs are marriage and family therapists at Central Texas Counseling & Family Therapy Center.

Relationships and Sexuality

by Eileen M. Raffaniello, Ph.D.

Parents often ask, "Do I really have to tell my kids about sex?" The answer is obvious—No, you don't have to *tell* your kids. Anyone whose child watches TV, looks at magazines, sees advertisements, or listens to the radio, knows that their kids have already been *told* about sex. Whether you talk directly to your children or not, they are getting messages about sex. The important question to ask is, "Do I want and need to talk with my children about sex, sexuality, sexual expression, and relationships?" Sexuality needs to be discussed within the context of relationships. Sexual expression is simply one form of relationships. Parents would be best served by recognizing that sex education is not a topic in and of itself, but a subcategory of a much more important category—that of intimacy and relationships.

Parents need to make sure that they give their kids accurate information, healthy sex-role models, and an understanding of positive, healthy sexuality. Parents communicate to their children by what they say and what they do not say, by what they do and what they do not do, and by their feelings, whether those feelings are expressed explicitly, denied, or acted out. Communicating all this to children is a very difficult task for parents and one that requires parents to become more conscious and more educated about their own understanding of sex and sexuality.

It is important to understand the differences between sex, sexuality, and sexual expression. Sex simply refers to gender. Sexuality, however, is a much broader term. Sexuality, the energy of our relating as either males or females to everyone and everything, can be defined many different ways, but I find it helpful to think of sexuality as our identification of ourselves as male or female, the way we relate to ourselves and other people, and the emotional responses we make to life. Sexuality is not an activity, but rather an affectional orientation toward ourselves, others, and life in general. Our sexuality develops over our entire lifetime. When talking with children, it is essential to provide them an understanding of sexuality as separate and distinct from direct sexual expression. Our sexuality—the way we understand ourselves and relate to others—develops and grows. Sexual expression is a result of the way we understand our sexuality.

How we talk to children may be even more important than what we say. We must be willing to answer questions when they come up—not later. Your kids might not ask again, and when questions aren't answered, the children get the message that this is a shameful or inappropriate topic. If it is impossible to answer the question immediately, tell the child that it is a good question and one that needs to be answered but right now you don't have the time or it is not the proper place. Set a specific time when you will get back to the question and *do* get back to it.

If you don't know an answer to a question that your child asks, admit it. Most of us don't have all the information we need. If you don't know the answer, don't give false information, don't make up an answer, don't evade. Admit that you don't know, and then go and get the information, either by yourself or with your child's assistance.

Feelings are an important part of any communication. When we talk, the message is not just the content but also the underlying feelings. In a conversation about our sexuality, it is easy to feel embarrassed. When dealing with the subject of sexuality, expect resistance and denial—your own and your child's. Remember that feelings that are denied get picked up by kids. As you talk with your children about any significant topic, remember to be in touch with your own feelings and express them as it is appropriate to the situation. If you are embarrassed, admit that you are embarrassed; your kids will know it anyway. Acknowledge the feeling and perhaps explain that this is because of some of the ways you were taught in your childhood. If your kids are embarrassed or confused, acknowledge their feelings. Validate the feelings; don't discount them. Then encourage your kids—and yourself—to move past the embarrassment so that you can have honest and important conversations.

Stay calm. If your child tells you something that you don't want to hear, don't explode. Really try to listen, to hear what is being said and not let your feelings get in the way of communication. Although we don't want to believe it, the reality is that many children in our culture are sexually abused. As with all abuse, one of the most dysfunctional things that happens is denial. If your child tells you he or she has been abused, be willing to listen and to act upon that information.

Watch for conversation starters. It is often hard for either parents or children to initiate conversation about sexuality. Since it is appropriate for parents to monitor TV and movies that children see, you can use these as opportunities to discuss topics that are presented—teenage sexual activity, pregnancy, marriage, relationships, divorce. All of these can be good starting points for a conversation. Ask open-ended questions: "What would you have done in that case?" "What do you think about that?" "How would you have felt?"

Remember to be positive whenever you can. Tell your kids what you think is healthy sexual expression and what are age-appropriate relationship skills. You can talk about how to make friends, how to express anger, how to handle conflict, how to express affection, how to set guidelines, how to make decisions. Emphasizing the do's will make the process more enjoyable for both you and your child. Don't stop with just one conversation. You can't have "the sex talk" and be done. You need to be in an on-going dialogue with your child about your child's relationship to self, friends, and family. Don't preach, don't lecture, don't diagnose, don't minimize, don't discount, don't fix, don't rescue. Do recognize and be clear and explicit about your own values. The most important facts you can communicate are your values. If you aren't clear, take the time to explore, clarify, and own your values about sexuality, relationships, and self-esteem.

Intimacy is one of the deepest human needs. Intimacy is the ability to let someone else know who you really are, what you want and need, and to be heard by them. Too often in our culture intimacy is reduced to and damaged by being seen only as direct sexual expression. Talking to your children about sexuality is actually educating them about intimacy. It can be an opportunity for growth for both of you.

Eileen M. Raffaniello is a licensed psychologist who does counseling and consulting in a variety of areas.

Drug and Alcohol Abuse: What Is Being Done?

by Bill Britcher

"Most Americans Say Drugs Are Top Problem" read the headline in hundreds of newspapers across the nation this week. Twenty years after the sounds of rock music and the smell of marijuana smoke intertwined defiantly over Woodstock, Americans have changed their minds about the use of drugs.

A recently released Gallup poll indicates that record numbers of adults and teenagers now agree that drug abuse is the nation's most serious problem. "The American people are in a wartime mode and sense a national emergency in the drug crisis," said pollster George Gallup at a White House news conference.

Two decades ago, a young generation tied experimentation with drugs to its search for love, peace, and good times. But now, the poll finds that most Americans of all ages associate drugs with danger, crime, and despair, with most favoring tougher drug laws and widespread drug testing. Furthermore, most respondents seem willing to take personal action, with about 75 percent of the teenagers and nearly half of the adults surveyed saying they would volunteer their time for drug prevention programs.

By a significant plurality, both teenagers and adults listed drugs and drug abuse as the nation's most serious problem. It ranked above fears of war, the economy, the environment, homelessness, AIDS, and a host of other concerns. "A record number of Americans cite the drug crisis as the nation's top problem, replacing the 'guns and butter' issues of international tensions and economic worries," said Gallup. "In the 50 years that the U.S. public has been asked to name the most important problem facing the nation, it is virtually unprecedented for any social issue to place at the top of the list."

Even a cursory look around reveals that there are too few alcohol and drug abuse prevention programs available to sway our young people away from the use of drugs. A closer examination reveals that treatment for adolescents is in extremely short supply, particularly if their parents aren't financially able to foot the bill for what can be very sizable treatment costs. Is there hope in sight?

Fortunately, today we can say that there is! Two major developments in the past few months have provided a "light at the end of the tunnel" for those searching for an answer to our problems. These developments are a major financial commitment from the Texas Legislature and the U.S. Congress and a new law providing for coverage of chemical dependency treatment under many Texans' health insurance plans.

The 71st Texas Legislature rose above their financial constraints to award the state's chemical dependency agency, the Texas Commission on Alcohol and Drug Abuse, an increase of $23 million over the next two years for programs for children and youth. These dollars will begin to fund a state-wide group of services that will include comprehensive prevention and intervention programs and treatment services designed specifically for youth.

These prevention and intervention programs are designed to prevent or interrupt the use of alcohol and drugs and focus on youth who are defined as being at-risk for drug use or as having a high risk of becoming addicted. These targeted youth include school dropouts, children of substance abusers, victims of abuse, pregnant teens, and those who have demonstrated repeated failures in school.

Treatment services provided under this new funding will include outpatient treatment services for those who can benefit from this less restrictive environment, which allows them to continue in school and in their normal surroundings. Residential treatment services will be provided for those whose addiction demands a more structured setting. TCADA will also fund institutional treatment services to address the special needs of youth who are in the criminal justice system. Throughout the funding process, special emphasis will be placed on programs that increase cooperation and linkages among the various public and private groups that are concerned with drug abuse.

The state's financial commitment to substance abuse services is now being augmented by increased funding from the federal government. Congress' passage of the Anti-Drug Abuse Act of 1988 provides for increased funding to fight the use and abuse of drugs. For the first time, substantial resources are being directed to reduction of the *demand* for alcohol and drugs through prevention, intervention, and treatment services. This is a significant change from the federal government's traditional focus on stopping the import of drugs at the nation's borders. This realization that demand reduction must go hand-in-hand with supply reduction holds great promise and will ultimately yield the best results. Much of the federal substance-abuse funding is targeted at programs to reduce the spread of the HIV virus which causes AIDS, since intravenous drug users are now the major cause of this virus' transmission.

The second major positive development in the fight against drugs is the passage by the Texas Legislature of SB 911, a new law which mandates coverage for treatment of all forms of chemical dependency under group health insurance plans and health maintenance organizations (HMOs). This new coverage, which will take effect on all policies written after January 1, 1990, expands the requirement for payment by insurance from alcoholism treatment to payment for recovery from addition to any drug.

The American public has listed alcohol and drug abuse as its number one concern. Fortunately, the public has been heard. More programs are being made available to curb the ominous spread of drug abuse, and now more sick people will be able to afford treatment so that they can once again be well and live happy, productive lives. There is, indeed, hope for dealing with alcohol and drug abuse.

Bill Britcher is Information Officer for the Texas Commission on Alcohol and Drug Abuse.

Traditional or Adolescent Orthodontics

by Albert H. Owen III, D.D.S., M.S.D.

Everyone knows that braces can straighten teeth, but the current scope of orthodontic treatment goes far beyond beautiful smiles. Orthodontic treatment includes improving the overall oral health, which leads to improved total body health. It won't be noticeable now, but in years to come, we hope to have improved your overall quality of life due to the various benefits that you may receive during orthodontic treatment.

Major orthodontic problems can exist in mouths that look very acceptable. If these problems are left untreated, they can severely jeopardize the health of the teeth, gums, bones, and jaw joints. Some of the most common problems include:

• Crowded Teeth—usually result from jaws that are too small. Crowded teeth are hard to clean, and this may lead to cavities or gum disease.

• Overbite—where the top teeth come way out over the bottom teeth. Bad overbites can cause excessive pressure on the front gums, or they can cause too much pressure in the jaw joints.

• Underbite—where the bottom teeth come out in front of the top teeth. Underbites usually do not chew food well and may cause digestive problems.

• Crossbites—where the back teeth are crossed over in reverse, creating imbalances in the bite and frequently causing the bottom jaw to shift to a strained position.

• Missing Teeth—sometimes we are born without certain permanent teeth, and the spaces they create need to be controlled, or else the adjoining permanent teeth will tip into the spaces.

• Jaw Joints—where the bottom and top jaws hinge together. Bad bites can cause excessive pressure in the jaw joints, which can lead to soreness, pain, and even impaired chewing ability later in life. Headaches are frequently the result of poorly functioning jaw joints.

To properly understand the particular type of problem and the extent of the problem, your orthodontist will need to take special x-rays of your jaws and skull, as well as molds of your teeth. As a teen, you are growing and changing every day, so an extensive knowledge of growth patterns and their tendencies is mandatory for the orthodontist to plan your treatment accurately. Because we are all individuals, your treatment will need to be individualized to gain the maximum results.

Due to extensive research, tremendous progress has been made in the types of orthodontic appliances in recent years. Your treatment may include the following types of braces or appliances:

• Retainers—are used to control local tooth problems or habits.

• Functional Appliances—can be used to correct bad overbites as long as you are still growing.

• Palatal Expander—may be used to widen your top jaw and teeth.

• Headgear—can be used to correct buck teeth or bad overbites.

• Braces—are used to place the teeth into a good bite. Braces come in lots of styles, but the trend has been toward smaller types. Clear braces made out of synthetic sapphire or a porcelain are also available today. Some doctors even use braces on the inside of the teeth so they don't show at all—but the technique is very difficult and hard to master.

• Extractions—sometimes removing teeth is necessary to make enough room so the remaining teeth can be properly straightened.

As everyone knows, orthodontic treatment improves bites, makes the teeth straighter, and makes smiles beautiful. Even though we only see the pretty smiles, the real benefits of straight teeth include:

• Improved balance and harmony between the top and bottom jaws
• Improved balance and function of the chewing muscles
• Ease of cleaning—which should mean less decay and fewer gum problems
• Improved chewing function—which means better digestion
• Improved balance and harmony of the jaw joints—which sometimes can eliminate headaches, as well as head, shoulder, and neck pains
• Improved self-esteem—which may be the most important benefit of all. A positive self-image is essential to feeling good and being confident about ourselves.

Look at the pictures. They show the teeth before and after orthodontic treatment. Consider the handicaps this patient would have had to endure if there had been no treatment.

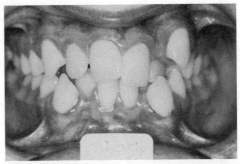

Before orthodontic treatment

The costs of various orthodontic treatment vary depending on the type of problem, the age of the patient, and the type of appliance used. Probably, orthodontic treatment is the best bargain in dentistry, regardless of the fee. Consider how many meals you will eat in a lifetime. If you live to be 70, you will eat around 70,560 meals, and if you are uncomfortable eating, then orthodontic treatment may be the best thing you can do for yourself.

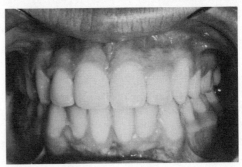

After orthodontic treatment

Albert H. Owen III is a board-certified orthodontist.

Preparing for Life Beyond Parenting

by Judy Barrett

Parenting is perhaps the toughest job anyone can do. It takes emotional and intellectual commitment, full-time attention to detail, large sums of money, and constant vigilance. In the course of doing the job, you find yourself—an otherwise intelligent and adult person—walking the floor in the middle of the night with someone screaming at you for no apparent reason, singing nonsensical songs in the middle of rush-hour traffic to keep down boredom or starvation, cheering for inept players of a game you never before cared about, watching performances of people who can't play the piano, dance, or do gymnastics and feeling stinging tears come into your eyes when the slips are made, and listening again and again to tragedies of skin condition, fatal hair-dos, and inappropriate clothing.

Through the years, you develop a split personality—you are no longer Jane or Joe Smith, but Jan or Johnny's mother or father. This person has definite responsibilities and chores in life—to drive the car, to fix the meal, to go to PTA meetings, Scout meetings, recitals, concerts, teacher conferences, and emergency rooms, and to write the checks. Your children need for you to be there, and you want to.

One absolutely necessary skill for parents that is never mentioned in parenting books is driving. Parents today spend most of their time with their children in the car—driving to school, to lessons, to day care, to friend's homes, on trips, and back home again. Once the kids are out of the car, they have other things to do—play, watch TV, study, eat, sleep. Most of the serious and hilarious conversations I've had with my children have been in the car. We're trapped there together and have to listen to each other. We've discussed sex, religion, politics, social responsibility, personal values, grades, and, of course, hair-dos while driving around town. On the highway, we've sung every camp song ever known, recounted our most embarrassing moment, confessed failures, and gloated over successes that we'd never get around to mentioning in the kitchen or living room.

But this alter-ego, the parent persona, does not just come to life in the car. This person permeates your entire life. No matter how active your social life, your career, your public role, Jan's mother or Johnny's father is always there worrying about niggling little things: "Is Johnny getting along with the new babysitter?" "Is Jan doing her homework?" "Are perfectly straight teeth worth the family farm?" Even the most casual parent worries about the grades, social success, emotional development, and general well-being of the child. You spend hours with people you don't particularly like because they are your children's friend's parents, or their teachers, or their coaches. You hear a cough in the middle of the night and think of things like pneumonia, consumption, and heroine addiction. Being a parent makes you inclined to excess—you spend too much, worry too much, sleep too little.

Then, all of a sudden, you're fired from this all-consuming job. The better you are at the job, the more definitely are you fired. Even if you're worn out from the job, can think of nothing better than your child leaving home forever, it still comes as a jolt. What do you do with all that driving experience? What do you do with the deeply ingrained sense that someone else is depending on you? What do you do with that other part of you that's defined by your child?

Of course, it doesn't happen all of a sudden. Early on, friends become more important than mom or dad. From at least 12 on there are definite signs of your coming obsolescence (and your present ignorance). When they're 16, you not only don't *have* to drive anymore, they will be happy to tell you that you don't even know *how* to drive! But it seems sudden—especially if you're a paragon of a parent—especially if you don't prepare yourself.

Giving up your children—letting them grow into independent adults—is, at the same time, the most satisfying and wrenching experience of a lifetime. You want them to be grown. You even want them to be gone. But you also want them to need you, to want you around, to confide in you, and to give you a sense of who you are. Just as you have gotten through those adolescent years and they are blooming into interesting and enjoyable people, they up and leave. It doesn't seem fair. Like caterpillars who sit around munching and making a mess for what seems like an eternity, they suddenly spread their lovely wings and fly away.

Well, it may not be fair, but that certainly is the way it is and the way it is supposed to be. The point is that you have to prepare for the transition. As hard as it may be, during all those years, you have to keep in the back of your mind that these people are just passing through. You're the one who's going to stick around. You're the one you've got to depend on in the clinch. You've got to keep nurturing yourself at the same time you're nurturing them. Keep up your independent interests—not just your job, but things you find sustenance in—books, other people, dreams, and private ambitions. These are the things you can return to with full energy when the kids are grown. But if you have let them go by the wayside during those years of active parenting, it's harder to revive them. If you let that parent person take over your entire life and become the only self you know, you're going to be in big trouble. Give yourself something to look forward to, something real and specific. And give yourself a break.

As your chicks leave the nest, you'll be constantly inclined to worry and fret over them. Give it up. They don't need it and you don't either. Grieve if you need to; most of us do. Shed some tears. Then get on with your life. There *is* life after kids, and if you think about it in advance, plan for it, and look forward to it, it can be great. Think about all the things you wanted to do but couldn't because of the kids. Think about how nice it will be to do them—even the little things. I still enjoy going into the bathroom alone, even though it has been several years since someone always had to go with me. I enjoy reading a book—not out loud. I enjoy watching TV programs of *my* choosing.

There is even life *with* kids after kids, but only if you let them be separate people, not your babies anymore. It's wonderful when you reach the point that you can be friends with your kids—good, supportive, money-lending friends. You can, in fact, be the best friend your kids will ever have. You don't *have* to be responsible for them, take care of them, feed or clothe them, but you can be supportive, loving, and a useful resource. You can just have a cup of coffee with them, talk with them about what they're doing and what you're doing. Reminisce about the old days together. Laugh about everyone's foibles together. And bask in the reflection of a job well-done.

Judy Barrett is a freelance writer and retiring parent of two daughters.

Central Texas Counseling & Family Therapy Center

  Michael J. Sliwa, M.A., L.P.C., provides diagnosis and treatment of children's, adolescents', and family problems. He is a specialist in academic problems (ADD, LD), emotional disorders, behavior problems, drug and alcohol abuse, and marriage and family discord.

  Michael Sliwa holds a master's degree in clinical psychology and has been in private practice since 1980. He is immediate past president of the Texas Mental Health Counselors Association and Membership Chair of the National American Mental Health Counselors Association. He is a consultant to At-Risk programs and juvenile probation departments. He is well known as a dynamic workshop leader in self image, parenting, and family relationships for school, business, and professional organizations.

  The office accepts MasterCard and Visa and is a CHAMPUS approved provider. The office staff will assist in filing insurance claims.

Central Texas Counseling & Family Therapy Center
13915 Burnet Road, Suite 205 • 244-7555
5100 Midway Dr., Suite 103, Temple • 817/773-0016
Hours by appointment

St. David's Adolescent Psychiatric Day Hospital

  The Day Hospital is a freestanding, partial hospital program for psychiatric treatment of emotionally and behaviorally troubled adolescents. It is a cost-effective program of intensive, medically supervised care for patients who can live at home during the course of treatment. The program operates Monday through Friday, providing an accredited school component, as well as individual, group, family, and therapeutic activities. It is designed for individuals from ages 12-18 and is administered by a multi-disciplinary team under the direction of a psychiatrist. Dr. George Willeford is Clinical Director and Dr. Michele Toth is Medical Director. Treatment is in an environment that fosters a family-like atmosphere.

  Out-patient care costs significantly less than full hospitalization and has the benefit of maintaining the family and social structure. The program is designed for young people who attend junior or senior high school; are suffering from anxiety, depression, behavioral problems, and conflicts involving family, school, or peers; need more intensive treatment than periodic office visits; have sufficient behavioral control to continue living at home; and have parental commitment to participate in a family therapy program. Patients are referred from physicians, psychologists, school counselors, families, and others. An initial consultation at no charge determines the appropriateness of a referral.

St. David's Adolescent Psychiatric Day Hospital
1000 E. 32nd, Suite F • 397-4100

Connie Young Benfield, Ph.D.

Dr. Benfield has had extensive training and experience in the outpatient treatment of families and children, as well as hospital inpatient evaluation and treatment of children and adolescents. Dr. Benfield began private practice in Austin in 1987 and specializes in diagnostic assessment and in individual, group, and family psychotherapy. Prior to that she initially was director of an outpatient substance abuse treatment clinic in rural Texas, and subsequently the clinical director of the inpatient treatment program of a private psychiatric hospital for children and adolescents. Dr. Benfield completed a Master of Arts degree in Psychology from Texas Tech University, which included a child/adolescent internship in an urban community mental health center; doctoral training for the Ph.D. in Psychology at Texas A&M University; and clinical psychology internship training at the University of Texas Health Science Center Medical School at Houston.

Connie Young Benfield, Ph.D.
7200 N. MoPac Blvd., Suite 160 • 338-1203

P. Caren Phelan, Ph.D.

Dr. Phelan is a family therapist who specializes in emotional problems, substance abuse problems, divorce and custody problems, and eating disorders. She provides custody evaluations, courtroom testimony, and custody mediation to facilitate better working relationships in joint parenting. A graduate of the University of Maryland, Dr. Phelan has done post-doctoral work at U.T. Austin and the University of Virginia. She has more than 20 years' experience with substance abuse treatment and spent two years in an intensive training course for family therapy. She uses a family systems-multi-generational approach to treatment that takes into account various family patterns that affect the individual. Specially focused group sessions are used in the treatment of adolescents.

A past board member of Austin Family House, Dr. Phelan is active in the local psychological association.

P. Caren Phelan, Ph.D. • Hours by appointment
7200 N. MoPac, Suite 160 • 346-6038

Austin Regional Clinic - Austin Mental Health Associates
Arbor Square • 12871 Research Blvd, #202 • 335-7084
Barton Oaks • 901 MoPac Expwy. South, #590 • 327-1713
Jefferson • 1600 West 38th, #404 • 459-4101

COUNSELING AND PASTORAL CARE CENTER OF AUSTIN
3701 N. Lamar, Suite 300 • 451-7337 • 1100 Round Rock Ave, Hwy 620, Suite 108
Founded in 1975 by Dr. William E. Denham, Jr.
Individual, marital, family & group therapy for children, adolescents and adults.

Beth Larsen, M.S.W., C.S.W.-A.C.P.
Psychotherapy (Children, Adolescents, Families)
3215 Steck Avenue, Suite 200 • 459-0739
Daytime, Evening & Weekend appointments available

JAMES MAYNARD, M.D.
3215 Steck Ave., Suite 100 • Austin, TX 78758
By appointment. Specializing in adult and adolescent psychiatry
458-9253

═══════ ❧ Substance Abuse ❧ ═══════

Charter Lane Hospital

Specialists in psychiatric care, Charter Lane offers quality inpatient and outpatient programs for children, adolescents, and adults. Their chemical dependency programs, which are firmly based on the 12 steps of Alcoholics Anonymous, are specially and separately designed for the different needs of men, women, and adolescents, and emphasize family involvement in treatment. Charter Lane also helps adults, adolescents, and children deal with problems of physical, sexual, and emotional abuse, behavioral and conduct disorders, eating disorders, depression, and many other emotional problems. A special in-house school with state-certified teachers specially trained to work with children and adolescents with emotional problems is available. Through treatment, patients are able to learn healthy coping behaviors and regain self-esteem. Upon discharge, weekly aftercare meetings and support groups are available.

Charter Lane Hospital
8402 Cross Park Drive • 837-1800 • 800/472-7422

Private Practice Physical Therapy Association Of Central Texas

All members of this group are members of the American Physical Therapy Association and subscribe to standards of ethics and guidelines of the Association.

Austin Physical Therapy Clinic •3215 IH 35/1107 Edgewood Ave. • 472-6238

Frankie R. Melder, P.T., received her physical therapy degree in 1959 from the University of Texas Medical Branch and is a board-licensed physical therapist. Her specialty is solving musculoskeletal disability as it relates to traumatic/repetitive injury and physical deformity. A wide range of conditioning programs are available for the return of adults/children to their normal levels of work/play.

Corley and Kelsey Physical Therapists • 3737 Executive Ctr. Dr., #200 • 346-2700

Ellen Corley, P.T., graduated from the UT Health Science Center at Dallas. Her special interests are foot/ankle, shoulder, and spine problems. Douglas Kelsey, P.T., graduated from State University of New York at Buffalo. His special interests include orthopedics (the spine and the knee). The office is open from 8 am to 7 pm Monday, Wednesday, Friday; and from 9 am to 6 pm Tues. and Thurs.

Georgetown Therapy and Rehabilitation Center • 805 W. University Ave., Suite C 863-0147 or 255-7883 ext. 399

Robert B. Wood, P.T., received his Physical Therapy degree in 1974 from the University of Texas Medical Branch in Galveston. The Center offers programs for both children and adults. Licensed professionals provide preventative and rehabilitative needs in the areas of physical, occupational, and speech therapy.

Su S. Lim, P.T. • 3215 Steck Ave., Suite 203 • 451-4348

Su S. Lim is a Physical Therapist, also registered with the state as a Massage Therapist, who specializes in pain management and restoration of physical dysfunction. She has training in Chinese herbal medicine, acupuncture, acupressure, and Japanese Shiatsu. She also has training in Temperomandibular Joint management, awareness through Somatic movement, and other techniques.

Donna J. Stoffa, P.T. • 5524 Bee Caves Rd., Unit J-1 • 328-0802

Donna Stoffa treats children from infancy to early adulthood who suffer from cerebral palsy, developmental delay, spina bifida, muscular dystrophy, learning disabilities, and attention-deficit disorders. She is trained extensively in Neuro Developmental Treatment and can provide in-home therapy. She has worked in home, nursing home, and school environments.

Jean Miller Tandy, P.T. • 4638 B South Lamar • 892-3521

Jean Miller Tandy graduated from the University of North Dakota at Grand Forks in 1980. She specializes in out-patient orthopedics, manual therapy, and wound and burn care. She enjoys treating children's orthopedic and sports problems because they heal so quickly. Her office is open 8-5 Monday through Friday and on weekends if needed for acute problems or wound and burn care.

The Therapeutic Group Incorporated • 4207 James Casey, #204 • 445-4988

Director Linda L. Park is a Licensed Physical Therapist who graduated from Texas Woman's University in 1975 with a B.S. degree in Physical Therapy. She has been in private practice since 1981. Her specialties include musculoskeletal conditions, sports injuries, and objective testing and screening. She is bi-lingual in English and Spanish. The office is open Monday through Friday, 8-5.

"Give your children your permission to grow up, to make their own lives for themselves independent of you, and independent also of your particular desires and ambitions. Give them a sense of truth; make them aware of themselves as citizens of a dangerous universe, a universe in which there are many obstacles as well as fulfillments, and prepare them for human nature in all of its varieties and forms and variabilities. Show them that they must anticipate in their lifetime pitfalls and snares and fickleness on the part of human beings from whom they could expect faithfulness. Do not make the mistake of giving your children a picture of the world that is painted in unrealistic colors in which there are lights but no shadows. Give your children a sense of proportion in the landscape of the world, a sense of the reality of life with its lights and shadows, of human nature with its goodness and its evils."

—Joshua Loth Liebman

CHAPTER VI

Adding to the Family

by Roy Cisneros, Jr., Grade 5, Ortega Elementary School

Special Pregnancies
by Byron G. Darby, M.D.

The majority of women who are pregnant and undergo childbirth are healthy, and their chances of developing problems with the pregnancy or with delivery are relatively low. However, a number of women fall into a high-risk category due to pre-existing health problems or problems that develop during the course of their pregnancy. With modern technology and skills, many of these problems can be overcome. Patients with chronic medical problems should have a thorough discussion with their physician of the relationship between their medical problems and the potential for increasing the risk of problems during the pregnancy. A brief discussion of some medical problems follows:

MEDICAL ILLNESSES

If a woman has a chronic medical condition, pregnancy may worsen her symptoms or the course of her disease. Examples of these conditions include diabetes, high blood pressure, heart conditions, lung problems, including asthma, liver or intestinal problems, multiple sclerosis, and lupus.

Babies born to mothers who have diabetes are at higher risk for birth defects and a number of other medical problems. It is most important that a woman who is a diabetic thoroughly discuss the risks of pregnancy with her physician before she attempts to conceive. It is also important that very strict control of blood sugar be achieved prior to attempting pregnancy or, failing this, as soon as possible after pregnancy occurs. Pregnancies in diabetic women require constant monitoring and testing. It is very possible, and even likely, that the woman will need to be hospitalized on one or more occasions during the pregnancy for control of her diabetes. Liberal use of ultrasound and non-invasive fetal testing, including monitoring the baby's heart rate frequently late in pregnancy, are essential to a good outcome. Premature delivery may be necessary when the mother is diabetic. This very close supervision and monitoring throughout pregnancy is often successful in achieving a healthy baby with minimal impact on the mother's long-term health outlook, and many diabetic women who years ago would have been told not to consider pregnancy are today giving birth to healthy babies.

Chronic high blood pressure is another significant risk factor for pregnant women. Close supervision of blood pressure and monitoring of the fetus throughout pregnancy is necessary. Patients with chronic high blood pressure often require premature delivery, but again, with modern management, a successful pregnancy outcome is often achieved.

Women who have the chronic medical conditions mentioned above are often able to have successful pregnancies, but all conditions should be thoroughly discussed with your doctor.

MATERNAL MEDICATION USAGE

Many women require medications for ongoing health problems, and fortunately, the majority of these cause no problems with pregnancy. However, a few drugs can be hazardous to the developing fetus, and any medication which the mother is taking should be discussed with her doctor, preferably before the onset of pregnancy, but certainly as soon as the patient discovers she is pregnant. In many cases it is far more hazardous for the mother to stop taking her medication and suffer worsening of her health problems than it is to continue the medication throughout pregnancy. A prime example of this is maternal epilepsy. Epilepsy medications have unfortunately been linked to birth defects; however, uncontrolled seizures during pregnancy carry a far higher risk of damage to the baby than the medications.

ILLICIT DRUGS AND ALCOHOL

Many illicit drugs, such as marijuana, cocaine, crack, amphetamines (speed), and LSD, have been associated not only with an increased risk of birth defects, but also in decreased growth of the baby and long-term mental and physical problems after birth. Cocaine and crack appear to be especially dangerous, and even one usage of cocaine or crack during pregnancy can cause severe brain damage to the baby. Any illicit drug used immediately prior to conception or during the pregnancy should be thoroughly discussed with your doctor.

Alcoholic drinks, including beer, wine, and liquor, have been associated with a number of problems during pregnancy when they are used on a regular basis. It appears that as few as two or three drinks every day can cause problems. On the other hand, there is very little evidence that a single rare social cocktail or beer causes significant problems. Nonetheless, it is probably prudent to totally abstain from alcohol during pregnancy.

SMOKING

Smoking is a very dangerous addiction. Women who smoke during pregnancy are at higher risk for miscarriage, birth defects, placental problems, smaller than normal babies, and a number of pregnancy complications. Infants of smoking mothers tend to have more respiratory problems, a higher instance of cerebral palsy, and developmental problems. Children of smokers have more upper respiratory infections and colds, and miss on average five more days of school per year than children of nonsmokers. Women who are pregnant should not smoke or, if unable to quit entirely, should cut back as much as possible.

ACUTE ILLNESSES

Everyone is susceptible to flu, colds, stomach viruses, and infections, and this is not different during pregnancy. Rubella (three-day measles), chicken pox, hepatitis, and a few viral diseases have been known to cause birth defects or fetal problems. Fortunately most viral or bacterial infections do not cause significant problems in pregnancy.

Acquired Immune Deficiency Syndrome (AIDS) is a very severe problem in pregnancy. AIDS syndrome in the mother often progresses very rapidly during pregnancy. Babies born to mothers who carry the AIDS virus often have a rapid progression of AIDS and die within months of birth. Women who are at high risk for having been exposed to the AIDS virus should talk to their physician about AIDS testing. High risk factors include a history of IV drug use, partners with a history of IV drug use, or bisexuality. Women whose partners have hemophilia also should have an AIDS test done. Blood used in transfusions is now tested for the AIDS virus. Until approximately 1987, however, the AIDS test was not available, and anyone who received a blood transfusion before this time probably should obtain an AIDS test as well.

EARLY PREGNANCY COMPLICATIONS

Approximately one in six recognized pregnancies end in miscarriage. The majority of these miscarriages are because the embryo did not form correctly. It is very rare for a miscarriage to be caused by factors over which the mother has control, such as exercise. A miscarriage is often a heartbreaking event, but women should remember that they should not feel guilty over a miscarriage since in most cases nothing could be done to prevent it. Bleeding in early pregnancy is relatively common, and fortunately, the majority of women who bleed early in pregnancy do not go on to have a miscarriage but are able to successfully carry the pregnancy to full term.

Ectopic pregnancy is a special type of abnormal pregnancy where the fetus is implanted in the fallopian tube or outside the uterus. This often produces symptoms such as abdominal pain and abnormal bleeding. Women who have a history of previous ectopic pregnancy, IUD usage, or pelvic (tubal) infections are at higher risk for ectopic pregnancies and should consult their doctor as soon as pregnancy is suspected.

FAMILY HISTORY AND MATERNAL AGE

A family history of genetic problems should be thoroughly discussed with your doctor. These family genetic problems could include hemophilia, sickle cell anemia, Tay Sachs, muscular dystrophy, cystic fibrosis, and spina bifida. Any history of a relative born with birth defects should be discussed with your doctor as well.

It is an unfortunate fact that a woman's age has a great impact on the risk of chromosome problems with the fetus. The most common chromosome problem is Down's syndrome. For example, the risk of a woman who is 25 of having a baby with Down's syndrome is approximately 1 in 1,400 whereas the chance of a woman who is 40 having a baby with Down's syndrome is approximately 1 in 100. Women who are 35 and over are usually offered the option of testing the baby for Down's syndrome if they desire. This testing is usually done by either amnio-centesis or a relatively new procedure called chorionic villus sampling. Amnio-centesis is usually done in the early second trimester at about 15 to 16 weeks of pregnancy and involves taking a small amount of fluid from the amniotic cavity around the baby. Chorionic villus sampling is performed at approximately 10 weeks of pregnancy and involves taking a small sample of the area where the placenta is forming, known as the chorion villi. Both chorionic villus sampling and amniocentesis can also be used to check for other genetic diseases. It is very important to discuss with your doctor any family history of genetic problems as early in pregnancy as possible, or even prior to pregnancy.

VAGINAL BIRTH AFTER CESAREAN SECTION

In the past several years it has become apparent that many women who have previously had a cesarean section are now able to successfully undergo a vaginal delivery with a subsequent child. As many as 60 to 70 percent of women can have successful vaginal births after cesarean births.

SUMMARY

Today a number of medical problems can be managed successfully. Often in the past, women with these problems were told not to become pregnant or that their chances for having a healthy baby were very poor. Today the outlook for women with these health problems is much better. Very careful discussion with your doctor and often extensive testing and follow-up throughout pregnancy are needed for optimal pregnancy outcome.

Dr. Byron Darby is an obstetrician and gynecologist who specializes in high-risk pregnancies, fetal testing, and genetics.

by Bumsoo Kim, Grade 12, Anderson High School

There Is Hope for Infertility

by Joe S. McIlhaney, Jr., M.D.

I got hugged by a patient yesterday. I performed an ultrasound scan of her uterus and showed the patient her tiny baby. This proved that not only did she have the pregnancy that she and her husband had so desperately wanted, but that it was a healthy pregnancy and, so far, a normal baby. This woman and her husband had, in the past, had four pregnancies all in her fallopian tubes, each requiring surgery for its removal. With the last operation, she was rendered sterile with both fallopian tubes finally being totally destroyed. She now had no chance of ever becoming pregnant—except for modern technology. In this patient's difficult situation, a normal pregnancy resulted from in-vitro fertilization. She hugged me yesterday because I had done the in-vitro procedure on her, and she was seeing the wonderful results.

Most couples who have difficulty becoming pregnant do not require procedures as technical as in-vitro fertilization (IVF). Whether a couple with a fertility problem requires IVF or a much simpler procedure, there is almost always something that can be done to help a couple be more fertile. All that is required is that a couple realize that they have a problem and then consult with a physician who has both the knowledge and the interest in helping them with their problem.

How do you know if you have a fertility problem? If you and your spouse have been unable to conceive a child after one year of normal sexual relations, you are considered infertile. This means that a couple who is having intercourse once or twice a week with no contraception should be pregnant within a year. If you realize that you have a fertility problem, you should see a physician. You should not put off this visit to the doctor. The longer you have a fertility problem, the worse it can become until you have actually become sterile. When you pick a physician to see for this problem, be sure that the doctor is one who is not only interested in problems of fertility but also knowledgeable about them. If you see a physician who tells you just to relax or to keep a record of your menstrual cycles and come back in six months or that no testing is necessary, you need to seek out a physician who is more informed about fertility problems and who will be more thorough in caring for you.

A couple is also considered infertile if they have been unable to carry a pregnancy long enough for a live birth. Two days ago I operated on a woman with a tubal pregnancy. This was her second tubal pregnancy, but in addition to this, she had had five miscarriages. This woman is infertile just as the woman who has never become pregnant. There are often tests and procedures that will help a woman with infertility of this type.

How many couples have fertility problems? A 1980 survey by the American Fertility Foundation indicated that 17 percent of married couples in the U.S. had some problem of fertility. This total number amounts to 3.5 million American couples. If you have a fertility problem, therefore, you are not unusual. Many people think infertility is always due to an abnormality in the wife. This is far from the truth. Studies show that infertility is caused by problems the woman has only one-third of the time. Problems with the man cause infertility one-third of the time. The final one-third of infertility is caused by problems that exist in both the husband and the wife.

What can you expect if you see a physician for infertility? First, you can expect the doctor to talk to you as a couple. There are many things that are relevant to a problem of fertility that a doctor can discover in talking to a couple. For example, one of my patients had a ruptured appendix years ago. This made me suspect that her fallopian tubes might have been damaged by her infected appendix. Subsequent studies did indeed prove this to be her problem. It is vital that your doctor sit down with you and talk, and it is important for you to give the doctor as much information as you can. At the end of the initial consultation, your doctor may not be able to tell you why you are infertile, but he or she will probably be able to lay out a plan of investigation for you as a couple.

If you are indeed infertile, your evaluation can be fairly complete in two or three months. This initial evaluation would include an analysis of the husband's sperm, an x-ray of the wife's uterus (called a hysterosalpingogram), laboratory studies for diabetes, thyroid disease, etc., and perhaps suggestions for taking basal body temperatures to detect ovulation. Very important in the evaluation of an infertile woman is a procedure called laparoscopy. If a couple has been infertile for two years or more, or if the woman is older than 35, the doctor may want to do a laparoscopy during the first two or three months of the evaluation. If the infertility has been present for only 12-14 months, or if the wife is less than 30 years old, the physician may feel that the laparoscopy can be delayed a few months.

Let us talk about some of the startling advances that have been made in the care of infertile couples in recent years. These new techniques truly do give hope to couples with infertility. A common procedure that is done today is the intrauterine insemination. If a couple has no obvious cause of infertility or has had some problems corrected and is still not able to get pregnant, this procedure can be helpful. On the day she ovulates, the wife comes to the doctor's office. She brings her husband's semen that he collected at home. The doctor uses a washing technique that gets rid of all the mucus and saves all the sperm from a semen specimen. He or she then puts a small plastic tube into the woman's uterus and pushes the sperm through the tube into the uterus. This technique is not magic, but has resulted in pregnancies in many women who had previously been infertile.

You may have asked, while reading the previous paragraph, how a woman knows when she is ovulating. This brings our attention to an amazing laboratory test that can be done by a woman on her own urine at home to tell if she is ovulating. By running this test on her urine during the days preceding ovulation, a woman can tell the day before she ovulates that she will be releasing an egg from her ovary in the next one or two days. This allows her to have intercourse at the right time or to have an intrauterine insemination done. This test also helps to prove that a woman is ovulating on a regular monthly basis—obviously a woman cannot get pregnant easily unless she releases an egg from her ovary on a fairly regular basis.

This brings us to a discussion of another miraculous tool that can be used in infertile women. The ultrasound scan technique that we used to see the baby in the pregnant woman we mentioned earlier is a technique that can be used to help couples achieve pregnancy—as a matter of fact, we used this technique with her. The ultrasound machine allows the physician to see a woman's ovaries. Not only can the doctor see the ovaries, but also he can see whether the ovaries are producing eggs. More than this, he can tell if the ovaries are releasing the eggs and when the eggs are being released. The physician can even tell when more than one egg is being released and can warn a couple that they might have twins or triplets.

A discussion of this type would not be complete without mentioning the great advances that have occurred with the use of laparoscopy. Laparoscopy is a relatively minor operation. It basically consists of inserting a telescope-like instrument through a one-fourth inch long incision in the edge of the belly-button. Often other, even smaller, incisions are made. With this technique, a woman's entire internal reproductive system is visible. Not only can the physician see these organs, but he can often treat problems that are present as well. A laser beam can be directed down the telescope. It can be used to evaporate endometriosis (a common cause of infertility). It can be used to cut adhesions. The laser can be used occasionally to open blocked fallopian tubes. Whenever these procedures can be done successfully, which is frequently, they save a woman major surgery.

Whenever we mention infertility and laparoscopy together, we are led to mention in-vitro fertilization. Laparoscopy has allowed physicians to gather eggs from a woman's ovaries without doing major surgery. Therefore, laparoscopy made IVF feasible. Now, however, the ultrasound machine can be used to "see" a woman's ovaries and can be used to direct a needle through the woman's upper vagina to retrieve eggs from those ovaries. This is even simpler than removing eggs with the laparoscope. Retrieval of eggs with ultrasound and needle requires sedation by an anesthesiologist, but it is a much easier procedure than it was in the past when the laparoscope was required. There are several other IVF type procedures. These include placing sperm and eggs into a woman's fallopian tubes (GIFT), placing fertilized eggs into a woman's tubes (PROST), etc., each having its place with couples with different types of problems. In addition to these procedures being easier than they were in the past, they are also much more successful. Expense does remain a major problem with these procedures—technology is expensive, but at least it is available, and perhaps with time not only will these procedures be easier but also cheaper.

The number of people in the U.S. who are infertile is increasing, so unfortunately the techniques we have been discussing will need to be used more and more. The number of infertile couples seems to be increasing for several reasons. Many couples are delaying childbearing to their later reproductive years when they are less fertile. Sexually transmitted disease has become the most rapidly increasing cause of infertility. (Sexually transmitted disease is a terrible scourge to people who have been infected but want to be fertile in the future.)

It is unfortunate that some couples will have to experience the pain of infertility. When I consult with an infertile couple the first time, I always tell them that frustration is almost universal among infertile couples. I encourage them with the fact that with modern techniques, with persistence, and with God's blessings, they have a fighting chance of seeing the exciting picture my patient saw—their own little baby, its heartbeat blipping like a light going on and off—on the screen of that astonishing ultrasound machine.

Dr. Joe McIlhaney is a gynecologist, obstetrician, and infertility specialist. He is the co-author of several books, including Dear God, Why Can't We Have A Baby?

by Melissa Cisneros, Grade 12, Johnston High School

Birthing Options

by Mary Ann Hazlett, BSN, MSN, ACCE

How will you welcome your baby into your family? Home or hospital? Doctor or midwife? Lamaze or Bradley? Natural, medicated, or by anesthesia? By investigating your options early in pregnancy or even before becoming pregnant, you will be able to make informed decisions with confidence. Your baby's birthday can be truly fulfilling.

Your investigation will include tours of all of the hospital facilities and birth centers and interviews with selected health care providers and childbirth educators. This should be done as soon as possible in order to find a birthing place and health care provider who share your own philosophy concerning childbirth so that you can work together to achieve a positive birth experience.

Aside from the occasional exciting taxi or car birth, babies are born primarily in three places: 1) Hospital, 2) Freestanding birth center, and 3) Home.

Hospitals offer three choices, although not every hospital offers all three. In the traditional labor and delivery area, the mother labors, delivers, and recovers in three separate rooms and is then transferred to a fourth room where she remains throughout her hospital stay. This type of labor and delivery area is used at the mother's and/or doctor's request and routinely for high-risk situations and for those mothers receiving anesthesia.

In the L-D-R or birthing room, the mother labors, delivers, and recovers in the same room and then moves to a regular hospital room for the remainder of her hospitalization. If the mother is given an Epidural anesthetic, she may possibly be moved to the delivery room for the birth.

The Alternative Birthing Center or Family Birthing Center offers the mother the opportunity of a home-like birth within the confines of a hospital setting where state-of-the-art medical technology is available. The mother labors, delivers, recovers, and stays in the center, along with her baby and partner, until hospital discharge time.

During the hospital tour you will gather useful information concerning rooming-in of infants, visiting hours, length of hospital stay and overnight accommodations for the mother's partner, and any limitations on the number of support people the mother may have during labor.

Freestanding birthing centers in the Austin area are run by midwives and are not affiliated with a particular hospital. Individuals who desire a home birth, but who do not live near a hospital in the event a transfer becomes necessary, may wish to consider this option.

Having your baby at home in your natural environment is the third option. Your care giver will be a midwife. As in the freestanding birth center and hospital birth center, family and friends may be present according to the mother's wishes.

In finding a health care provider most suited to you, you may need to interview several doctors and/or midwives. Remember that you are hiring them. Your time, effort, and possibly your money will be a good investment in future satisfaction. Your objective will be to find out where the person practices, his or her usual methods of practice, how he or she feels about preparation for childbirth, and exactly what choices you have. You will want to become acquainted with the midwife's transfer procedures and know who the back-up physician is in case hospitalization becomes necessary. An interview with that physician will also be helpful to you. In the hospital your midwife will assume the role of labor support.

Childbirth education classes are offered in a variety of places—hospitals, churches, recreation centers, doctors' and midwives' offices, and at the home of the instructors. You will want to find out your instructor's educational background, type of certification, experience, approach to childbirth education, and willingness to refer you elsewhere for additional or different training.

Four major types of childbirth preparation classes are: 1) Lamaze, which emphasizes a conditioned response to labor involving relaxation, breathing, and concentration, 2) Bradley, which is highly consumer oriented, advocates natural childbirth via relaxation, 3) Hospital preparation, which informs parents what to expect at that particular hospital, and 4) Home Birth preparation. A good class would incorporate elements of all four.

A thorough preparation will cover the physiology of labor, how the mother will feel both physically and emotionally, how the mother and her partner can use self-help tools to birth naturally, and also how they can cope with labor aided by medical technology. Advantages and disadvantages of any method should also be covered. Complications, along with their usual treatments, including Cesarean birth, will also be addressed. An emphasis on flexibility will help in coping with the unexpected. The length of a class series typically ranges from four to ten weeks (once a week for a few hours). Hospital preparation and Lamaze classes are usually four to six weeks. Bradley and home birth preparation classes are usually eight to ten weeks.

In natural childbirth the mother uses a combination of self-help techniques such as relaxation, breathing, concentration, and massage to work with her body to give birth. This method relies heavily on the mother's motivation and attitude, and on a supportive partner, nurse, and birth attendant (doctor or midwife). Some mothers may find that hiring professional labor support (montrice) is extremely beneficial in helping her and her partner work together.

In addition to or instead of self-help tools, a pain medication such as Demerol can be used to help the mother relax and cope with labor more effectively. The epidural anesthesia is available to those mothers who do not wish to feel their contractions. Self-help tools are not needed after the anesthesia is administered as the mother is then numb from her navel usually to her mid-thighs.

With thorough education, planning, and a positive attitude you will be able to create and shape the birthing experience most suited to your personality.

Mary Ann Hazlett is staff nurse in the Brackenridge Hospital Alternate Birth Center and parent educator in the Wellness Program.

Robert Casanova, M.D.

Dr. Casanova graduated from Tulane University with a degree in psychology and then attended Southwestern Medical School in Dallas. He did his residency at John Peter Smith Hospital in Ft. Worth. He is board eligible in Obstetrics and Gynecology. Dr. Casanova has staff privileges at St. David's.

Dr. Casanova believes strongly in providing information for his patients to help them learn and understand how their bodies work, how to correct problems, and what treatment options are available. He helps patients make informed choices. He works with new parents in dealing with problems that arise after delivery and is available and willing to talk with his patients about any problems in their lives. He provides a comfortable environment and enjoys spending time with his patients. He encourages fathers to be involved in the pregnancy and delivery of their children.

The office accepts MasterCard, Visa, and several insurance plans. They will file insurance claims for hospitalization and delivery.

Robert Casanova, M.D.
805 East 32nd • 472-5570

Jo Bess Hammer, M.D., F.A.C.O.G

A graduate of Baylor University, Dr. Hammer attended Baylor College of Medicine and served her residency at Baylor College of Medicine Affiliated Hospitals in Houston. A Diplomate of the American Board of Obstetrics and Gynecology, a Fellow of the American College of Obstetricians and Gynecologists, and a member of the American Fertility Society, she offers basic OB/GYN care. She also works with fertility problems and enjoys working with adolescent girls.

A mother of three, Dr. Hammer empathizes and understands her patients' needs. She pays attention to the emotional and psychiatric side of life and will refer patients to therapists when she feels it would be helpful. She also refers patients to other physicians when necessary. She works with women from adolescence through menopause. Dr. Hammer has staff privileges at St. David's Hospital and likes to have family members involved in the birthing process when possible. She always explains procedures and developments to her patients. The office accepts MasterCard, Visa, and American General PPO, and will file insurance for hospitalization and delivery.

Jo Bess Hammer, M.D., F.A.C.O.G.
805 East 32nd St. • 477-1954
Open Tuesday - Friday, 8-4:30, One Saturday Morning per Month

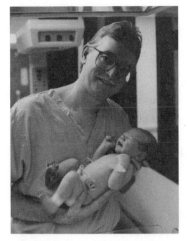

Jeffrey Youngkin, M.D.

Dr. Youngkin received a B.A. with honors from UT Austin and attended Baylor Medical College for his M.D. degree with honors. He served his residency in obstetrics/gynecology at Baylor, where he was chief resident his last year. He opened his practice in Austin in 1982. He is a Fellow of the American College of OB/GYN, a member of the American Fertility Society, and a member of the Society of Reproductive Surgeons. Dr. Youngkin offers general care in obstetrics and gynecology with an emphasis on infertility. He is one of only four Austin doctors who do in-vitro fertilization. Practicing exclusively at St. David's Hospital, he works with adolescents through senior citizens and will work with children referred by pediatricians. Dr. Youngkin provides his patients with educational information and keeps them informed and well-advised about what to expect in pregnancy and other treatments. He encourages fathers to participate fully in the pregnancy and birthing experience. Dr. Youngkin helped design the new LDR (labor, delivery, recovery) rooms at St. David's.

Jeffrey T. Youngkin, M.D.
805 East 32nd, Suite 202 • 478-3188

Mark Akin, M.D.

Dr. Akin received his B.E.S. in engineering from UT Austin, his M.S. in Bio-Medical Engineering, and his M.D. from UT Southwestern in Dallas. He served his residency at Parkland Hospital in Dallas and opened his practice in 1983. Dr. Akin provides complete obstetrical, gynecological, and infertility care. He delivers only 10-15 babies per month, focusing more on the quality of care than on the quantity of patients. He delivers over 90 percent of his own patients, and his C-section rate is much lower than the national average. Prenatal classes are taught in the office by a nurse with six years' experience at Seton labor and delivery. All prenatal testing and lab work is done in the office. Infertility care, including ovulation induction and laser microsurgery, is of special interest to Dr. Akin, comprising over 30 percent of his practice.

Mark Akin, M.D.
1301 W. 38th • 451-8211
Open Monday — Friday, 8-5

Vernon L. Elledge, M.D.

Dr. Elledge graduated from the University of Texas Medical Branch in Galveston and served his internship and residency at Parkland Memorial Hospital in Dallas. He began private practice in Austin in 1966. The primary focus of his practice is on annual physical exams, including pap smears and pelvic examinations. He also does surgery when needed, obstetric care, and works with infertility problems. He uses the hysteroscope to evaluate menstrual problems, and provides sonograms, non-stress tests, and lab work in the office. Dr. Elledge takes delight in helping a woman have a normal delivery and encourages the husband to act as the labor coach. He takes time to discuss options and answer questions with all of his patients.

Vernon Elledge, M.D.
1301 West 38th St., Suite 109 • 451-8211
Open 8—5, Monday, Tuesday, Thursday, Friday

Patricia A. Gunter, M.D.

Dr. Gunter received her M.D. degree from Baylor College of Medicine, as well as doing her residency there. Her private practice opened in Austin in 1988. She is board eligible, and utilizes St. David's and Brackenridge Hospitals for delivery and gynecological procedures.

Dr. Gunter strives to make patients feel comfortable and at ease and combines a balance between objectivity and sensitivity in her practice. She encourages and supports a natural approach to childbirth, and welcomes requests and participation of both parents. She offers current procedures with a special interest in infertility. Dr. Gunter believes in providing patients with enough information and guidance to make their own health care decisions. The office accepts MasterCard, Visa, and most insurance plans.

Patricia A. Gunter, M.D.
1015 East 32nd, Suite 200 • 474-1043
Hours by Appointment • Office open 8-5, Monday — Friday

Cindy J. Mingea, M.D.

Dr. Mingea received a B.S. in pharmacy from Auburn University and received her M.D. degree and post-graduate training from Baylor College of Medicine, Houston, Texas. She is board eligible. She was in private practice in Tennessee before choosing to relocate in Austin.

Dr. Mingea strives to establish a good rapport with patients. She provides patient education to help create a more informed patient who is prepared to play an active role in achieving and maintaining her good health. Children are welcome in the office. Fathers-to-be are encouraged to participate in pregnancies, from prenatal visits through delivery. She provides a very family-oriented environment for health care.

The office accepts MasterCard and Visa and may accept certain health plans. The office is open 9-5, Monday, Wednesday, Thursday, and Friday.

Cindy J. Mingea, M.D.
900 East 30th, Suite 201 • 479-6655

Christopher Glenn Seeker, M.D.

Dr. Seeker received his M.D. at the University of Texas at San Antonio and served his internship and residency at Baylor Medical Center at Dallas. He has staff privileges at Seton, St. David's, and Brackenridge Hospitals. Dr. Seeker provides obstetric and gynecological care with a special emphasis on infertility problems. He manages prenatal care and deliveries, and encourages the father to participate in the entire process from doctor visits to prenatal classes. Dr. Seeker teaches prenatal classes and develops a close rapport with his patients. His wife meets the parents during classes and often visits them in the hospital after delivery. A very low C-section rate is a point of pride with the doctor, as is the effort made to make each visit to the office pleasant and comfortable.

Christopher Glenn Seeker, M.D.
1301 West 38th, Suite 109 • 451-8211
Open Monday — Friday, 8-5; Thursday, 8-12

Emilio M. Torres, M.D.

Dr. Torres received his B.S. degree from Rice University and graduated from Baylor College of Medicine in 1980. He served his internship and residency at Baylor College of Medicine. He is board certified in Obstetrics and Gynecology.

Dr. Torres offers OB/GYN care and strives to include the patient and family as much as possible in the care. He provides a great deal of education material and takes the time to make sure patients understand their options and treatment. He works with infertility problems and is open to delivery requests, always keeping the health of baby and mother as a first priority. Dr. Torres is multi-lingual and is affiliated with St. David's, Seton, and South Austin Hospitals.

Emilio M. Torres, M.D.
900 East 30th, Suite 214 • 476-1941

Austin Regional Clinic - Obstetrics/Gynecology
Central Austin • 1301 West 38th, #205 • 451-6811
Medical Park • 1301 West 38th, #201 • 451-6910
South Austin • 4007 James Casey, #C-150 • 444-8886

JOE S. McILHANEY, JR., M.D.
811 EAST 32ND • 476-7766
Specializing in gynecology and infertility
A founder and practicing physician in the in-vitro program at St. David's Hospital

Brackenridge Hospital Alternative Birth Center

The Alternative Birth Center (ABC) enables families to be as close as they would be during home delivery, while maintaining the support and security of an expert medical staff trained in prepared childbirth. The specialized ABC staff is trained in relaxation and support techniques. Medications are available if needed. The ABC is also prepared for any unexpected problems. Each birthing suite consists of a fully furnished living room and bedroom, a large queen-size bed, and a wooden cradle for the new arrival. Following birth, the baby stays with you, and the whole family can fall asleep together. Any family members or friends may be present before, during, or after delivery, depending on your wishes. Tours of the ABC are conducted weekly. Childbirth classes are available.

Brackenridge Hospital Alternative Birth Center
601 East 15th St. • 480-1916

PROGRESSIVE PARENTING WORKSHOPS
Raise a more responsible child • Increase your child's self-esteem
Discipline without punishment • Manage the strong-willed child
473-3860

ST. DAVID'S HOSPITAL PARENT EDUCATION PROGRAM • 397-4226
Informal, friendly & personalized. R.N. instructors certified in area of expertise.
Early Pregnancy Classes • Lamaze • Cesarean • VBAC
Diabetes & Pregnancy • Lamaze Review • Breastfeeding • Baby Care

SETON PARENT EDUCATION • 465-3131
Classes on labor and delivery and special concerns
such as basic care and breastfeeding.
Maternity and sibling tours offered for you and your family.

The Casey Family Program

A licensed, privately endowed children's agency, The Casey Family Program provides quality, planned, long-term foster family care for children and youth. Both boys and girls ages 6-15 years of all ethnic backgrounds are referred when long-term foster care is the plan of choice.

The Casey Family Program originated in Seattle, Washington in 1966 and has been operational in Austin since 1985. It is one of 15 established divisions nation-wide designed to serve children who are unable to live with their families and for whom adoption is unlikely. The goal is to provide optimum growth and development experiences for children in a foster family setting. Programs include services to both the children and the foster parents. Foster parents receive training and support before and during foster care. They are always looking for families to parent older children. The office is open Monday - Friday from 8:30 to 5:30.

The Casey Family Program
4701 West Gate Blvd., Suite E-502 • 892-5890

by Jessica Rogers, age 9, Austin Montessori School

"*Every child from its conception is a potential personality, though that personality may be nipped in the bud by some accident, deformity, or mental deficiency which from birth or later may limit its development. No one, not even parents well acquainted with their family history, can foresee with assurance, the ways in which the potentialities of a normal infant may unfold, because of the multiple strands of its physical and psychical inheritance from its thousands of more remote ancestors.*

"*The parents must protect the child's bodily welfare, train him to good habits, awaken and guide his sense of right and wrong, and nourish his mind with the cultural traditions of mankind. They may encourage him to acquire a wholesome self-reliance, or may unwisely warp his mind into conformity with their own prejudices, but they can never wholly determine for him the ways or the measure in which, as he advances into manhood, he will make use of what is given him, for his alone is the chief responsibility for the personality which he will develop in his intercourse with his fellow-men throughout the years of his life.*"

—from *The Religion of an Inquiring Mind*
Henry Wilder Foote

CHAPTER VII

Special Help for Special Situations

by Miguel Ortiz, Grade 1, Sanchez Elementary School

Coping with Your Child's Handicap

by Dianne H. Tannreuther, M.S., OTR

We all want our children to be born perfect. We want them to grow up, achieve new skills, learn many things, and develop into independent, well-adjusted, and happy adults that are able to face the challenges, obligations, and imposed demands of life. We want them to develop physically, mentally, emotionally, and socially. Raising a child is probably one of the most important and rewarding, though overwhelming, challenging, and frustrating tasks. Having a child with a handicap makes that task even more difficult for a parent.

In some children, the problem may be apparent at birth. In many other children, the difficulties may not show up until much later. A learning disorder may not be apparent until the child has entered school. You, your child's pediatrician, or someone else may first observe the problem and recommend testing. A child may have problems in some or all areas, including physical development, cognitive functioning, emotional control, and/or social skills.

Many parents go through the stages of grief (denial to acceptance), and feelings may vacillate between hope and despair. At first, there is often a period of guilt, projecting, and blaming. This is a difficult time for both parents. A period of isolation often comes next. This isolation may range from separation from other parents and family members to isolation from each other. In whatever stage a parent is, there is often a great deal of anger, maybe directed at yourself, the medical profession, the educational system, and even your child. This anger, frustration, and hopelessness needs to be brought out into the open. All parents will eventually come to some sort of acceptance of their child's problem, and in many instances, fathers and mothers will handle it differently. Many couples often find they are in different stages at the same time, but the parents must share the pain and work toward reasonable solutions.

There are many services available for a child with a handicap. The earlier the problem is detected and services begun, the better for the child. Programming may even start as soon as possible after birth. Programs are available through various city, county, and state-funded programs, as well as from local school districts and private therapists, agencies, and facilities. The type of problem your child has will help to determine what programming options are available for you and your child. Probably the best person to ask for advice and help initially is your child's pediatrician. Your child's doctor may also want to refer you to another physician or some other professional for further testing. You will also probably find that there are numerous approaches and treatment methods for your child's problem.

Getting the correct diagnosis for your child often helps a great deal. Knowing why or how a problem happened, however, is sometimes a mystery. Sometimes the reasons will never be known.

The role of parenting a child with a handicap often becomes easier as the parent becomes involved in the child's progress and program and learns that there are still many possibilities. Learn all that you can about your child's problem as well as about normal growth and development. A parent may also need to become an "educator," primarily to other family members, relatives, friends, the child's teacher, or the therapist. Family and friends will often want to help, but do not know how or what to do. Your child will also need you to be his advocate. Although there are many things you can do for and with your child, do not take over all of the role of "teacher," because your child first and foremost needs "parents."

Many parents find that attending a parenting class is quite helpful. These classes, whether geared toward normal development, parenting, or discipline techniques, are often a good source for information as well as a way to meet other parents. Many of the programs in which your child may be enrolled have parent support groups. Getting to know other parents and discussing how they deal with the problems is probably one of the best ways to help you cope. Other parents will help you learn what resources are available, and they can tell you what works and what does not from their experience.

As with any child, especially a child with a handicap, expect normal behavior as much as possible. Your child may often need more time, extra help, and repetition to learn new things, but the child can learn. Repetition is often critical. As a parent, you will probably get tired of doing the same thing over and over again long before your child does. Let the child do what he can, especially when it comes to being a participating family member. Although your child may have special problems, try not to treat him or her differently. Help your child be more independent. As with any child, take one day at a time and enjoy all of your child's accomplishments. Accentuate your child's strengths and help him or her compensate for the weaknesses.

Dianne H. Tannreuther is an occupational therapist with the Children's Evaluation and Therapy Center.

by Brooke Atherton, age 11, Kirby Hall School

Family Law
by Melissa Wiginton

"The first thing we do, we kill all the lawyers."
—William Shakespeare

That Shakespeare's suggestion is almost universally accepted demonstrates an equally universal resistance to the prospect of dealing with lawyers and the law. The family lawyer has the additional challenge of dealing with life's most feared subjects: death and divorce. While one article cannot undo years of "lawyer phobia" or reverse natural human instinct, an understanding of a few basic concepts can make family law issues more approachable.

Many people have heard that Texas is a community property state. According to the Texas Constitution, community property is all property acquired during the marriage other than separate property. What is separate property? It is property which is a gift to either the husband or wife, inherited by either husband or wife, or owned by either spouse before the marriage. The characterization of property as community or separate is significant upon both death and divorce.

The most important legal consideration for all families is the disposition of property and the care of children in the event of the death of one or both of the parents. If one parent should die without a will, each piece of community property would be divided equally between the surviving spouse and the children, with the children's share being administered through a court-supervised guardianship. Such a guardianship requires filing an accounting of how the property has been used each year until the children are grown. The expense and legal entanglement of a guardianship can be easily avoided with the preparation of fairly simple wills. A will can create a trust, tailored to the parent's desires, in which assets can be held and used for the children's benefit until they are grown. Such a trust can be administered by a trustee without court supervision. Parents can also name the guardians of the children.

The significance of a community property is also important during divorce. The divorce is a dissolution of the marriage partnership between husband and wife, and in many ways it is treated like the dissolution of a business partnership. Assets and debts must be identified, characterized as to whether they are separate or community property, and valued.

Each party is entitled to retain ownership of his or her separate property. In fact, the court does not have the power to award one spouse the other spouse's separate property. The court may, however, recognize claims of reimbursement between the separate and community estates. If the parties made payments out of their jointly earned income for a mortgage owed by the husband before marriage, upon divorce the community would be entitled to be repaid for payments made less any benefits received by the community. The right to reimbursement is an equitable one—one which is based on fairness.

The law in Texas specifically requires a division of community property which is just and right. So, courts begin with the proposition that community property should be divided equally between husband and wife. An equal division does not necessarily imply that each party will receive half of each asset and pay half of each debt. Rather, equal division will result in each party taking away from the marriage a combination of assets and debts with a total value equal to one-half of the net value of the total community estate. An equal division is not always a fair one, however, and the court will consider many factors. The relative earning capacities of the parties, fault in break-up of marriage, status of health, size of separate estates, who will have custody of the minor children, and any other circumstance which a lawyer can bring before the court will be considered by the judge in assessing whether a disproportionate division of community property is more fair than an equal division.

It is important to remember that a divorce court does not have the power to affect the rights of a third-party creditor. That means that a court cannot order a creditor to release one spouse from liability on a joint debt. So, if one spouse is awarded a car on which there is a lien in both parties' names and fails to make the payments, the lienholder can seek satisfaction from either or both parties. The spouse who was not awarded the car cannot use the fact that he or she does not have possession to avoid the obligation.

Finally, every divorce suit in which children are involved includes a Suit Affecting the Parent-Child Relationship. The Texas Family Code makes provisions for a child's needs through rules regarding custody, visitation, and support. In Texas, the parent who has primary possession of the child and most of the rights, powers, duties, and privileges of a parent is called the Managing Conservator. The parent who has possession of the child only during specified periods is designated the Possessory Conservator. In general, the Possessory Conservator has the duty to supply the child with food, clothing, and shelter during times of possession and the power to consent to medical treatment during an emergency. Both parents always have equal rights and access to medical and educational records of the child. Parents may also be Joint Managing Conservators. Specifics regarding time spent with each parent, financial arrangements, and the allocation of decision-making powers vary depending on the needs of the individuals; however, every decree which names parents Joint Managing Conservators must state which parent will choose the residence of the child or where the residence will be. Joint custody arrangements are designed for the least impact on the child's routine. Judges closely scrutinize all proposals with that in mind.

The Legislature has also passed guidelines for use by courts in setting the amount of child support to be paid. A percentage will be applied to the amount of net resources of the person paying support to arrive at a dollar figure for support. Net resources is generally defined as gross income less Social Security and income tax withholding (one exemption) and the cost of health insurance. The support obligation continues only until the child reaches age 18 or graduates from high school.

As children grow, their needs change. Therefore, the custody, visitation, and support decisions made at the time of the divorce can be changed by further court proceedings until the children are adults.

When the time has come that legal assistance is needed, remember that the law arose to meet the needs of the people. Not only is the law set up to work for families—so are lawyers. Fortunately, in the area of family law, most practitioners are sensitive to the family's needs and able to assist clients through the process without undue trauma. Lawyers are necessary helps in the system.

Melissa Wiginton is an attorney practicing in family law in Austin.

Effective Single Parenting

by Patti R. Ricker, CSW/ACP

As a single parent, you are head of one of the 8.8 million single-parent families in the United States (one-fourth of all families in the U.S., according to the last U.S. census). You may experience yourself as isolated, but it is estimated that up to 50 percent of families will be headed by single mothers in the 1990s.

Guilt

Guilt is the number one problem that interferes with effective single parenting. Guilt for not being able to accomplish more; for not providing another parent in the home; over scarce money; for having needs and worries; and for taking time to care for yourself plagues single parents. How does this affect parenting? Inappropriate or excessive guilt leads parents to overindulge children and to have difficulty setting limits. It leads to feelings of stress and lowered self-esteem, which may result in being harsh and impatient. So, you have a combination of permissiveness and harshness which confuses children.

It is important that you hold yourself accountable for mistakes, but forgive yourself and stand firm as a parent. Doing this on your own is difficult. Use friends as consultants to help get perspective. Delay decision making until you can get outside input and support. Be aware that guilt makes you vulnerable to your children's pain and their desire to be pleased. Remember that giving in to demands does not make up for past or current losses, and being harsh does not help your child learn from mistakes.

Love and limits

Love and limits combine for effective parenting. Focus on the love and approval you feel toward your children and share it with them. Discipline is effective when the child is secure in your love. This is especially important for children who have experienced loss such as divorce or death. Focus on positive behavior whenever possible. Have family meetings and discuss things that work well in the family. To discipline, use logical consequences and try to add chores instead of taking things away. Take classes to learn about child development. Many are available in Austin for low fees, and most provide child care.

Taking care of yourself

Many parenting mistakes result from too little time and too many unmet emotional needs on the part of parents and children. Take good care of yourself, and you will be better able to care for your children. Exercise, a healthy diet, relaxation, time with friends, and time alone will help you be an effective single parent. Do not expect your children to take the place of adult companionship in your life. They cannot substitute for intimacy with adults. You have needs separate from your children. Learn your strengths and weaknesses. Make goals to improve your ability to handle finances, household chores, relationships, and parenting.

Remember to ask for help. You don't have to go it alone. Agree with a friend to be on call 24 hours a day to help with emergencies. You need to know that someone is available when you need help.

Have extra cash stashed away for emergencies. Make car repair your number one priority. Get help with budgeting from a knowledgeable friend or from a community class.

Myths about single parenting:

Myth #1—"Single parenting is a crisis."
Divorce is a crisis. Single parenting is a lifestyle. Don't put your life on hold until you marry, waiting for the addition of a spouse to create a family atmosphere or a sense of completeness to your family life. Don't delay home improvements, vacations, or parenting and lifestyle decisions. Live life one day at a time, creating a sense of family with traditions and routines. This gives your children a sense of "this is the way we do it in our family." Children need this structure, continuity, and identity as a family.

Myth #2—"You can do it all."
Parenting on your own is a big job and requires assessment of expectations of yourself in all areas. Evaluate roles and chores, dropping or reassigning those that can be taken over by someone else or left undone. You cannot be both mom and dad to your children; it is physically and emotionally impossible. In the case of death or divorce you cannot change the fact that one parent is no longer in the home. This must be acknowledged and grieved. Utilize support people: friends, family, neighbors, teachers, church, and co-workers. Your children can take over some household tasks and can provide you with occasional emotional support. Be careful that your expectations don't exceed their developmental abilities or force them to give up too many of their childhood activities.

Myth #3—"You are all alone."
The feeling of being alone is very real and can be overwhelming. Utilize support groups, neighborhood co-ops, and parenting classes geared toward single parents. Ask for help; don't wait for it to be offered.

Myth #4—"Single parenting is all bad."
Single parenting can be fun and at times easier than sharing daily parenting. You can make decisions and carry them out on your own, giving you confidence and self-esteem. You may experience more closeness with your children. Creative problem-solving and self-reliance are modeled for the kids, and they learn skills useful in adult life. You may also enjoy the time away from the kids if they visit their other parent. These are some of the unique aspects to single parenting. It is a lifestyle full of challenge and reward. You can do it effectively!

Patti R. Ricker is a CSW/ACP, a Diplomate of Clinical Social Work, and Family Life Education Specialist at Child and Family Service.

by Evan Ferlet, age 8, Wesley School

New Relationships After Divorce: The Effects on Children

by Larry Miller, Ph.D.

Divorce brings about many changes in the families it affects. The changes involve both the adults and the children. Many of the adjustments are viewed similarly by both the adults and the children, either as "good" or as "bad." When there is the feeling that "we're all in this together," the changes are easier to manage. When something comes along that the parent sees as good and the kids see as bad, then the process is much harder to manage for all concerned. Such is often the case when a parent begins to date or enters into a serious relationship.

The divorce process

The process of divorce begins long before the actual granting of the divorce decree. And it clearly doesn't end there. It begins well back into the marriage relationship when the fighting, or the isolation, or the sense of not being oneself is so pronounced that dissolving the marriage becomes a real option. It progresses through the time of actual separation, the day in court, and even through the possible remarriage of one or both of the parents. There are periods (which may last for years) of single parenting where both the children and the custodial parent (usually the mother) have to learn to live together in a different arrangement. This is no small task. Learning to live without a parent involves a great deal of struggle for most single-parent families. After a while, however, new patterns are developed, new roles learned. Things settle down. The children and the parent have largely been "on the same side." That is, they have had mutual tasks that required mutual cooperation to master. After years of upset that may have existed during the marriage and immediately following separation and divorce, things become relatively calm again.

New relationships

Just when things seem to calm down, a new person may enter the picture, mom's boyfriend or dad's girlfriend. This event often seriously divides the children and the parent. The parent will view this new relationship as being good, a sign that life is going forward. To the children, however, this new person may well be seen as an unwelcome intruder, a threat to the status quo. The presence of a new man or woman may dash the hopes of the children for the reconciliation of their parents (a fantasy that most children have). The parent will most likely spend a good deal of time with his or her new friend and less time with the kids. As a result, both the parent and the friend may be the recipients of a great deal of anger and attempts to sabotage the relationship.

In stark contrast to the scenario spelled out above, there are children who welcome a new man or woman into the "family." For them, the new person is not an intruder or a rival, but a longed-for parent substitute or just an adult friend who can be a playmate, buddy, or mentor. When this happens everyone concerned is a winner. Unfortunately, this situation is more the exception than the rule.

How to deal with the problems

First, it is important to realize that almost any change may be resisted by the children in the beginning. Given time and sensitive handling of the introduction of the new person into the family situation, much of the initial resistance is likely to fade. Most of the time, the problem is not with the new person, per se, but with the idea of another person in the picture. So, be patient and understanding.

Second, while the adult need not get (or seek) permission from children to date, it is an activity that does affect the children, so they need to be involved in the process at some point. Just when and how depends on the ages of the children and the seriousness of the relationship. There are no firm rules as to just when a new date should be introduced to the children or when the children might be included in an activity. When the children can get to know the new person and realize that he or she does not pose a threat to their own relationship with the parent, the problem will be reduced significantly.

Third, it's quite possible that the trouble with the children may cause trouble with the new relationship. He or she may need patience and understanding too. If this person is unable or unwilling to "tough it out" until things get better, he or she may not be the person to get very serious about anyway.

Finally, it's you who are caught in the middle of the whole mess. You have needs and desires as an adult, and you are sensitive to the needs of your children. How you handle this issue may well set the stage for how you handle other issues with your children where you and they have different perspectives. Ultimately your adult decisions are yours alone to make. It is not good for you, or ultimately good for your children, for them to play a major role in decisions that they have neither the experience nor the authority to make.

Larry Miller is the founder and director of the Divorce Recovery and Family Resources Center, P.C.

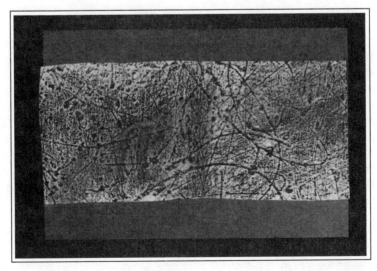

by Amanda Boni, age 5; Tiffany Hoffmann, age 5, Children's Discovery Center

Facing the Realities of Stepparenting

by Anna Gonzalez-Sorensen, Ph.D. and Don M. Sorensen, Ph.D., CSW

The challenge of stepparenting

Stepparenting is different from parenting in the traditional nuclear family. The stepparents and stepchildren come from different backgrounds, have had different life experiences, and may have different values. A stepfamily often is formed while some members continue to experience and confront the losses resulting from the ending of a previous primary relationship. In addition, the stepparent finds himself or herself an "instant" parent to children whom he/she has not had the opportunity to know and love from their birth.

Relationships among all stepfamily members must be developed; they are not a given as is the case in the nuclear family. In the case of divorce, the step-parent must contend with the influence of a biological parent who resides out-side the newly formed stepfamily. Consequently, these complexities, while extremely challenging to the parents in a stepfamily situation, can offer the promise of a rewarding, nurturing, and fulfilling life for everyone. This article points out the unrealistic expectations many parents bring to a new stepfamily situation, the more likely realities they will encounter, and some guidelines for working through the challenging task of creating a happy, harmonious, and nurturing environment for everyone.

Common unrealistic expectations and the realities

The most prevalent unrealistic expectation is that there will be "instant" love among all members of the newly formed family. The reality is that loving relation-ships require a long time and a lot of effort to develop. Love does not happen automatically. Because some members of a stepfamily do not get to choose who they want to live with, they may, in fact, never come to feel "love" for other members of the new stepfamily. Nevertheless, it is reasonable to expect that stepfamily members can learn to accept and respect each other.

A second unrealistic expectation is that the children will feel as excited and as happy as the parent and stepparent who have just married and are "in love." The reality is that often children are still feeling the pain of loss of their original nuclear family, as well as feeling guilt, anger, and confusion about being in a family not of their choosing.

Other unrealistic expectations are that the newly married couple will be in total agreement regarding discipline, and that the children will respond positively to the discipline provided by the stepparent. The reality is that often the couple discovers that they have very different requirements for what constitutes accept-able behavior and appropriate responsibilities for the children. The children need time to develop a stepparent-friend relationship so they can become more willing to accept the discipline from the stepparent. Older children have a more difficult time accepting the authority of an "outsider." They often rebel and refuse to accept the new family unit.

Another unrealistic expectation is that the newly formed stepfamily will recre-ate the former "family" situation that was lost, "only this time it will be better." The reality is that the new family unit cannot and will not replace the lost former family. The new stepfamily is different in many ways, including the structure, the influence of others, and the increased number of potential interactions with extended family members. Essentially, the newly formed family unit may not necessarily be any better or any worse, but it will definitely be different.

These unrealistic expectations are often the cause of unnecessary stress and conflict. Therefore early recognition and correction of these erroneous beliefs will accelerate the process of stabilizing the stepfamily. The guidelines that follow are suggested to help stepparents develop relationships with stepchildren so that the stepfamily can integrate more smoothly.

Some guidelines

• It is of primary importance that the couple make a firm commitment to make their relationship their first priority. This means that the remarried couple establishes a strong bond that can withstand pressures that come from within and outside the home. Establishing a strong bond requires the couple to take the time and energy to know each other well by learning to discuss all aspects of their relationship before and after marriage.

• If either partner was in a former relationship, he or she needs to work on healing and completing the emotional disengagement from the former partner.

• The process of integration of the stepfamily requires time, patience, knowledge of parenting skills, and energy.

• Open communication is the foundation for building the trust that is necessary for a successfully functioning stepfamily. Active listening by the parents helps the children develop trust and increases their feelings of belonging in the new family unit. Parents and stepparents need to become askable parents, those to whom children feel safe asking questions.

• Family meetings, regularly scheduled, are a means for family members to communicate their feelings, needs, and desires, and to negotiate getting them met. Family meetings also provide an ideal format for establishing family expectations and fair rules for dividing up chores and other responsibilities. These meetings also provide an opportunity for the family to be together to play or to share in some positive community experiences.

• When children visit the non-custodial parent, it is important to understand that possibly they will be experiencing feelings of sadness, guilt, fear, etc., and therefore, they may need quiet or alone time before leaving and/or just after returning from the visit. They often need this time to re-enter gradually and deal with whatever they are feeling. Parents need to be available, but not intrusive.

• Adolescents are in the process of "breaking away," so it is important to remember that this may mean that they are not interested in family cohesion. They often rebel as they try to establish their own individuality and identity.

• Children need time to establish a friendship with the new stepparent before they are willing to accept discipline from him or her. This process of relationship development must be gradual and cannot be forced.

• It is helpful to remember that feelings are temporary. They do not last forever. If Mary is angry, the feeling lasts only for a short while, then she goes on to feel the next feeling. Parents, therefore, need to have patience and acceptance of the wide range of feelings expressed by their children.

Anna Gonzalez-Sorensen and Don M. Sorensen are family counselors practicing in Austin.

Grandparenting in the '90s

by Martha Perkins

So now you are holding your grandchild for the first time—or is it your fifth or tenth? What an opportunity for you to make a difference in a child's life! What awe—what joy—remembrances all flash through your mind. You are a "Grandparent in the '90s!"

Is grandparenting different now from what you remember as a child? My grandparents were the stereotyped Victorian couple in the "gingerbread" house. Grandfather was stern but fair, distant but hard-working. Grandmother was always available—cookies and love—but she had very set standards: little ladies do not say "golly" because it is coarse, and my brother should not mow the lawn without a shirt on because ladies could see him "half-naked."

How do we grandparent today when profound changes have resulted in the following:
• Any words and actions seem readily accessible on television or elsewhere.
• Many children are kept in daycare centers from birth on because both parents are working.
• Many grandparents are unavailable for regular sitting for a variety of reasons.
• Family get-togethers on holidays are often characterized by "fast food" or prepared foods, with much time spent before the television set. Little time is made available to visit. "Back when," basic tasks of hunting or gathering food, preparing and processing food, washing dishes, sewing, and other forms of household chores provided built-in opportunities to know and to enjoy grandparents.
• Multi-marriages and divorces produce many combinations of parents and relatives, making a confusing and often emotional mess for all the family.
• All of us are flooded with conflicting messages of how we should look, act, and be.
• Deeply held beliefs and customs have been severely challenged.
• We have learned that many time-honored concepts of child-rearing used by well-meaning, but uninformed parents have been shown to be cruel, abusive, and mentally and physically damaging to children and adolescents. A brutalized child passes brutality on to others.
• Hectic family schedules do not permit kids to "hang out" with other kids or even family members, especially grandparents.
• Modern technology has freed many of us from drudgery, helped us to live longer and better, and provided a constant flow of information and entertainment. Yet many children are surviving, but not thriving.

What is needed from grandparents in the '90s? Basically what you and I and all children have always needed—to be nurtured. What does that really mean? Let's look at it from a child's point of view.
"I need to be seen and accepted for who I really am."
"I need to be loved for myself, not for what I may become, achieve or perform for someone else, i.e., not for my grades in school, my achievement in sports,

the money I make."

"I need to be helped to unfold little by little and become who I am."

"I need to be allowed to make mistakes, to explore, to experiment, to act silly without fear of ridicule or shame."

"I need models and standards and spiritual values."

"I need to have limits and boundaries firmly and lovingly enforced."

"If I'm allowed to be me, then I am not imprisoned by false values and senseless rules, but can find my own fire and passion to achieve that which I came into the world to do or to be who I came to be."

"I need a person who can make time for me—real "quality" time, and that means when I can feel free to be me, to talk about me from "deep-down.""

"When I am mad, afraid, unhappy, or crying, I need someone who does not get angry with me for feeling these things. He or she helps me understand why I feel a certain way and helps me learn how to cope with it. This person helps me learn about fear and courage, death and life, love and sexuality. This person helps me learn how to keep going, even though a lot of life seems unfair. She or he helps, not by telling me what to do, but by understanding, empathizing, and sharing his or her own experiences of the challenges of life."

In conclusion, we as grandparents can choose how we want to be with our grandchildren. Some of us are not cut out to be grandparents. It's not easy to love stepchildren and the assorted acquired relatives that are now part of so many families. On one thing most grandparents agree: when they see their children doing the same things they did and belatedly realized were mistakes, it is hard to know when to keep our mouths shut and when to speak "words of wisdom." The important thing to remember is the child's need for support and love. The grandparent of the '90s can be that special person who takes the time to share and care.

Martha Perkins has thirty years' experience as a teacher, counselor, and parent educator, and has two grandchildren. She is director of The Listening Tree.

by Sean McArthur, Ryan McGehee, Helen Hutka, Berkley Palm, and Caroline Deats, all age 3, Wesley School

William R. Jacobs, Ph.D.

Dr. Jacobs offers diagnosis of child development focusing on educational development, including reading disorders (dyslexia) and attention deficits (hyperactivity), and makes recommendations for treatment. He works with ages three through adult. A graduate of the University of Texas with a Ph.D. in Learning Disabilities, Dr. Jacobs holds a masters degree in Behavioral Disorders. He has been in practice for 14 years and is also a certified regular and special education teacher in the state of Texas. He has published tests for pediatric assessment and journal articles dealing with learning disabilities. He also directs a special Summer Learning Institute, assisting children with a wide range of learning support for fostering school success. Payment plans and insurance are available.

Austin Children's Clinic of the Austin Diagnostic Clinic
3410 Far West Blvd., Suite 100 • (512) 338-4098
Northwest Pediatrics at Seton • 11111 Research Blvd., Suite 150 • (512) 338-5150

Austin Regional Clinic - Learning Evaluation Program
Learning Disabilities & Special Education Therapists
901 MoPac Expressway South, Suite 590 • 327-9132

"We are mindful that within each child exists an immense potential that emerges as the years pass—and that we realize with some apprehension that the quality of our own lives will determine how well this potential is realized in full bloom and flower."
—Fred A. Cappuccino

Pediatric Therapy Services

Founded in 1983, Pediatric Therapy Services currently has a staff of 11 therapists. All have extensive backgrounds in pediatrics. The therapists have completed thorough training in the evaluation and treatment of children with neurological impairments and developmental delay. The staff includes physical and occupational therapists and speech/language therapists. PTS provides evaluation, direct treatment, consultation, and parent education/support for children birth-21 years of age who are diagnosed as having sensory integrative dysfunction, development delay, learning disability, neuromuscular disorders, genetic disorders, and orthopedic problems. Owners are Deanna Engber, OTR; Carole Harkavy, LPT; Bobbi Sargent, M.S., C.C.C.; and Beverly Veltman, LPT.

Pediatric Therapy Services
1601 W. Koenig Ln. • Austin • 453-0037
901 Round Rock Ave., Suite 300 • Round Rock • 244-0529

Donna J. Stoffa, P.T.

Donna Stoffa has a B.S. in Physical Therapy and received her certification in Physical Therapy from Albany Medical School; she is also certified in the neurodevelopmental treatment approach to cerebral palsy. Donna has continued to receive education and training in pediatrics and has provided therapy in many settings involving adult and pediatric care. She has been at her current location since 1987.

Donna Stoffa treats children, from infancy to early adulthood, who have cerebral palsy, developmental delay, spina bifida, muscular dystrophy, learning disabilities, and sensory integration dysfunction. She works closely with the family and encourages family participation in the therapy. Donna's goal is to make the treatments both functional and fun. She strives to help her clients maximize their potential.

Donna J. Stoffa, P.T.
5524 Bee Caves Rd., Suite J-1 • 328-0802

AUSTIN CENTER FOR SPEECH, LANGUAGE AND LEARNING
Martha McGlothlin, Director, Speech-Language Pathologist CCC
Evaluation, Therapy, & Tutoring for Toddlers through Adults
3810 Medical Parkway, Suite 153 • 450-1177

CHILDREN'S EVALUATION & THERAPY CENTER
12501 Hymeadow, Suite F • Austin, TX 78750
331-5488
Occupational, physical, speech therapy, audiology

Central Texas Audiology & Speech Pathology
2525 Wallingwood (MoPac at Bee Caves) • 327-6179
Evaluation, Consultation & Therapy
Experienced certified staff • Infants—Adolescents

BLUNN CREEK SCHOOL
1711 Sylvan Drive • 442-5557
Full program integrating the disabled with normal children Ages 1-14
Director has B.A. in Child Development/Special Education; Full & Part Time After School

OPEN DOOR
Three Convenient Locations • 477-9632
Infants through Pre-school • 7:30-5:30
Mainstream childcare for disabled and normally abled children

══════════════ ⚹ Attorneys ⚹ ══════════════

Paul T. Morin, P.C.

Paul Morin received his B.A. degree from Southwest Texas State University and his law degree (J.D.) from the University of Texas. He is licensed to practice by the State Bar of Texas and the United States District Court for the Western District of Texas. As an independent practitioner, Paul offers personal service. You will not have to deal with an assistant when you need legal advice. The firm is a general civil practice designed primarily for individuals and families. Services include adoption, guardianships, wills, divorce, child custody, and support. The firm can also handle personal injury, consumer rights, and other problems with the law that a family might face. Saturday or evening appointments are available if needed

Paul T. Morin, P.C.
6836 Austin Center Blvd., Suite 120 • 343-1299

Vika Newsom

A graduate of the University of Denver and the University of Texas Law School, Ms. Newsom has been in practice in Austin since 1985. Since that time she has concentrated on Family Law. She handles wills, probates, guardianship, real estate as related to estates, and divorce. Ms. Newsom tries to help her clients see both sides of an issue so that negotiations are fair and reasonably conducted. She is a member of the American Family Mediators Association and the Austin Family Mediation Association, and is a volunteer mediator at the Dispute Resolution Center of Travis County. Realizing that people are at their most emotional during divorce, she attempts to keep a calm perspective and encourages participants to deal reasonably and fairly with each other. She works with therapists to refer clients, if needed, and encourages participation in post-divorce support groups.

Vika Newsom
811 Nueces • 322-9191 • Mon. — Fri. 8-5

Austin Kids Xchange, Inc.

Kids Xchange provides a peaceful environment where children of divorced parents can be picked up and dropped off for visitation. The goal is to remove the child from situations of conflict and power struggles between parents. Kids Xchange provides divorced parents with neutral ground. At Kids Xchange, supervisors and counselors are available to work with families and give parents assistance to enhance the well-being of their child. Services include exchanges, controlled visitation, supervised visitation, documentation, confidentiality, testifying with subpoena, and counseling. Mike Wilkinson is director of the organization. Office hours are Tuesday-Friday, 10-6. Exchanges and visitations are scheduled by appointment and include evenings and weekends.

Austin Kids Xchange, Inc.
503 Oakland Ave. • 472-3588

MOVING THROUGH—BASIC TOOLS FOR DIVORCING PARENTS
Melissa Wiginton, Attorney, and Mary Fogel, L.P.C. • 452-3327
One-day workshop for parents considering divorce, divorcing, or divorced; Constructive ways to deal with legal, emotional, and parenting issues involved.

by Sam Carr, age 5, Lake Austin Montessori

The Listening Tree

The Listening Tree is a counseling center for personal, family, and organizational growth. The counselors work with couples, families, and children who are experiencing difficulties in their lives due to crises, stress, transition, relationship problems, or chemical dependency. Through a balance of careful listening and caring feedback, they help clients clarify their feelings, come to terms with their situation, and create new choices in place of old patterns. The staff is comprised of highly qualified, caring professionals experienced in counseling, teaching, and consulting with people of all ages. They draw on a diverse range of disciplines to assist clients in resolving difficulties and expanding their capacity for learning and growth. They also work closely with medical and other community services when appropriate. Martha Perkins, founder and director, has 30 years' experience as a teacher, counselor, and parent educator. She and other staff members offer seminars and workshops on a wide range of topics, including stress, change, anger, depression, self-esteem, and others. The staff includes Tom Zimmermann, M.A., L.P.C.; Ellen P. Zimmermann, M.A., M.F.C.C., L.P.C.; Victoria Sullivan Hendricks; Marie Welsch, Ph.D.; and Bill Woodburn, M.Ed. Call for an appointment.

The Listening Tree
3906 N. Lamar • 458-2844

Kathy A. Sheley, Ph.D.
Austin Family Center

Dr. Sheley views problems from a systems perspective; that is, she asks what multiple factors currently influence the problems a patient is experiencing and simultaneously tries to coordinate efforts toward the most workable aspects of the problems and of potential solutions. She does both inpatient and outpatient therapy and assessment, and works both with recent and chronic difficulties in psychotherapy, helping people to learn from current relationship difficulties to avoid similar future experiences. Because of a wide variety of certification and training, Dr. Sheley can treat the whole family, either individually or together. She uses individual and/or family therapy to assess and treat different problems.

A Health Service Provider in clinical psychology, Dr. Sheley opened her practice in Austin in 1980. She is an Approved Supervisor for the American Association for Marriage and Family Therapy and a Certified Sex Therapist. She did her residency at the University of Texas Medical Branch at Galveston and taught for two years at the U.T. Health Science Center in San Antonio. Dr. Sheley's office is centrally located one block west of MoPac North. Clients seen by appointment.

Kathy A. Sheley, Ph.D.
5926 Balcones Drive, Suite 215 • 453-6688

Marlowe Helen Donaldson, M.D.

Dr. Donaldson's primary interest is psychotherapy with children, adults, families, and couples. She will prescribe medicine if necessary, but is conservative in her use of medicine. She works with preschool through adolescent age children. She has a play therapy room for younger children and works primarily with outpatient care. She is conservative about recommending hospitalization for young people and is sensitive to families' spiritual needs and concerns.

A graduate of Rice University, Dr. Donaldson graduated from the University of Texas Southwestern Medical School in Dallas in 1973. She took a seven-year leave of absence to stay home with her children. After serving her residency in general psychiatry at UT Health Science Center in San Antonio, she received an Austin State Hospital Child Psychiatry Fellowship at Children's Psychiatric Unit. She is available for consultation by appointment.

Marlowe Helen Donaldson, M.D.
925-B Capitol of Texas Hwy. South, Suite 250 • 328-7313

Carlos M. Loredo, Ph.D.

Dr. Loredo provides therapy, consultation, and psychological evaluations for children, adolescents, adults, and families. He is bilingual and received his Ph.D. from the University of Texas at Austin in 1977. He was licensed as a psychologist in 1978 and has been a practicing therapist since that time. Dr. Loredo has seen clients with a wide variety of issues and has special training in sexual and physical abuse. He has an energetic style and actively participates in his clients' therapy. Over the years, he has also enjoyed working with numerous community agencies, such as The Settlement Home, The Casey Family Program, Junior Helping Hand, Austin Child Guidance Center, Child and Family Service, and Waterloo Counseling Center. His practice is located in South-Central Austin.

Carlos M. Loredo, Ph.D.
2111 Montclaire • 443-0190 • Open 8-6 Monday - Friday

Kathy T. Rider, C.S.W., A.C.P.

Kathy Rider is a board-certified Clinical Social Worker who provides therapy for adults, couples, families, children, and adolescents. She is also certified as a family mediator and holds group therapy sessions for women and for men and women. After serving on the staff of Austin-Travis County MHMR for eight years and the faculty of the School of Social Work at UT Austin for four years, she opened her private practice in 1981. She is adjunct professor at St. Edward's University in the Social and Behavioral Science department. Her orientation in therapy is to the family and the total environment in which the person lives. She sees her role as helping people help themselves.

Kathy T. Rider, C.S.W., A.C.P.
3724 Jefferson, Suite 206 • 452-8938
Monday — Friday, 8:30-5:30, Thursday evening until 9

Cathey J. Roberts, M.D.

Dr. Roberts does assessment and psychotherapy for children, adolescents, and adults. She is conservative in her use of medication and does long-term therapy, family therapy, and play therapy. A graduate of Rice University, she attended the University of Texas Medical School at San Antonio and served her internship and residency in adult psychiatry at the UT Health Science Center in San Antonio. She received a fellowship in child psychiatry from the University of Texas Health Science Center in San Antonio. She served on the staff of the UT Austin Student Health Center from 1983 to 1985 and opened her private practice in 1983. She evaluates children in the context of their family situation and offers an evaluation session with parents before beginning any treatment.

Cathey J. Roberts, M.D.
3724 Jefferson, Suite 221 • 453-8681
Office open 10-6:30, Monday - Thursday, 8-2, Friday

P. CAREN PHELAN, Ph.D.
7200 N. MoPac, Suite 160
346-6038
Hours by Appointment

EILEEN M. RAFFANIELLO, Ph.D., P.C. licensed psychologist
individual • couple • family of origin/family systems • relationship • women's issues • sexuality • spirituality • counseling & consultation • workshops & lectures
11130 Jollyville Rd. • 338-4404

Anna Gonzalez-Sorensen, Ph.D. and Don M. Sorensen, Ph.D., C.S.W.
4131 Spicewood Springs Rd., Suite C-5 • 345-8195
Individual • Couple • Family • Stepparenting • Biofeedback
Divorce Recovery • Stress Management • Codependency Recovery

THE DIVORCE RECOVERY & FAMILY RESOURCES CENTER, P.C.
Larry J. Miller, Ph.D. • 4101 Medical Parkway, Suite 105 • 459-9511
Therapy, Support Groups, Workshops, Seminars
For children & adults regarding separation, divorce & becoming single again

Sylvan Learning Centers

Sylvan is a group of neighborhood educational centers offering reading, math, writing, study skills, algebra, college prep/SAT/ACT, and school readiness programs. They test in order to pinpoint the specific areas in which a child needs help. Sylvan then attacks the problem with an individual program designed to fit the student's needs. Positive motivation, friendly encouragement, an experience of success right from the start, and a certified teacher who provides individualized attention make all the difference. The student's learning skills and self-esteem will improve dramatically.

Sylvan Learning Centers
Far West 346-0215 • Anderson Mill 335-1286 • Brodie Oaks 441-3898

BIOFEEDBACK TRAINING CENTER
Tom Kubiszyn, Ph.D., Director
11130 Jollyville Rd., Suite 300 • 338-0728
By appointment weekdays, weekends & evenings

"Nothing is strange to the child for whom everything is new.
Where all things are new nothing is novel.
The child does not yet know what belongs and what does not;
*   therefore for him all things belong.*
The ear of the child is open to all music.
His eyes are open to all arts.
His mind is open to all tongues.
His being is open to all manners.
In the child's country there are not foreigners.
                                    —from *This World, My Home*
                                    Kenneth L. Patton

"Your children are not your children.
They are the sons and daughters of Life's longing for itself.
They come through you but not from you,
And though they are with you yet they belong not to you.

"You may give them your love but not your thoughts,
For they have their own thoughts.
You may house their bodies but not their souls,
For their souls dwell in the house of tomorrow, which you cannot visit,
*   not even in your dreams.*
You may strive to be like them, but seek not to make them like you.
For life goes not backward nor tarries with yesterday."

—Kahlil Gibran

CHAPTER VIII

Resources

by Jennifer Houston, Grade 5, Ortega Elementary School

ALCOHOL AND DRUG ABUSE
Al-Anon Family Group	441-8591
Preteen Al-Anon	288-1011, 288-1444
Alateen	267-1322
Austin Drug & Alcohol Abuse Program	447-2327
Austin Family House	441-2086
Austin-Travis County Alcohol Counseling Services	473-9533
Austin Women's Addiction Referral & Education	322-0125
Greater Austin Council on Alcohol & Drug Abuse	926-4511
MHMR-Austin Travis County	447-2055
Parents in Recovery	478-1648
MADD-Mothers Against Drunk Driving	338-9410
SADD-Students Against Drunk Driving	338-9410
Texas Commission on Alcohol & Drug Abuse	463-5510

ANIMALS
Animal Control-City	469-2024
Animal Control-County	473-9825
Humane Society of Austin	478-9325

BETTER BUSINESS BUREAU
476-6943

BIRTH & DEATH CERTIFICATES
469-2085

COMMUNITY SERVICES
American Red Cross	928-4271
Austin Women's Center	447-9666
Car Seat Lender Programs (infants-6 mo.)	458-7405, 458-7402
Caritas Health Clinic	459-6002
Dispute Resolution Center	443-5981
Goodwill Industries	472-6224
Salvation Army	472-2628
United Way/Capital Area	478-7176

EMERGENCIES
Ambulance, Fire, Police	911
Poison Control	478-4490

FAMILY SERVICES
AFDC - Food Stamps North	929-7350
AFDC - Food Stamps South	444-5463
AFDC - Medical Programs North	929-7350
AFDC - Medical Programs South	444-9515
Austin Families Inc.-Childcare Switchboard	454-4732
Big Brothers & Big Sisters, Inc.	440-8811
CEDEN Family Resource Center	477-1130
Central East Austin Community Organization	472-5575

Resources

Child Assault Prevention Project (CAPP)	458-6303
The Child Care Connection	345-3900
Child & Elder Abuse Hotline	800-252-5400
Child & Family Services Inc.	478-1648
Child Inc., Child Development Program	451-7361
Children's Protective Services (DHS)	834-0034
Center for Battered Women	385-0620
Day Care Licensing Office	835-2350
Extend-A-Care, Inc. (After-school care)	454-3651
Family Outreach / Capital Area	459-4833
Family Outreach / Williamson County	869-2665
Infant-Parent Training Program	472-3142
La Leche League	836-9060
Lutheran Social Services of Texas Counseling and Adoption Services	454-4611
Marywood Maternity & Adoption Services	472-9251
Parents Anonymous	478-9922
Parents Warmline	477-9276
Parents Without Partners, Inc.	459-5573
Pebble Project-Child Abuse Center	454-4722
Planned Parenthood of Austin	477-5846
Runaway Hotline	463-1980, 800-392-3352
Teenage Parent Council of Austin	473-8825
Travis County Children's Protective Services	834-0034
WIC - Women, Infants & Children Austin-Travis County Health Dept.	474-1526
Youth Employment Service	479-6248

HEALTH SERVICES

AIDS Services of Austin	472-2437
American Diabetes Association	322-9292
American Heart Association	451-5135
American Lung Association	343-0502
Arthritis Foundation-Capital Area Branch	451-7323
Austin Children's Cancer Center	479-8538
Caritas Clinic	459-6002
Center for Attitudinal Healing	327-1961
City-County Health Dept.	469-2008
Family Asthma Program	480-1607
Hospice Austin	458-3261
Leukemia Society of America, Inc. (San Antonio)	737-1777
Medical Assistance Program	469-2030
Mental Health Association in Texas	476-0611
Natl. Foundation March of Dimes	328-3463
Ronald McDonald House	472-9844
State Health Dept.	458-7111

TEL-MED - Taped Health Information	473-4107
Texas Medical Assoiation.	477-6704
Texas Society to Prevent Blindness	338-9668

LEGAL SERVICES

Attorney General-Child Support Division	463-2005
County Attorney	473-9415
District Attorney	473-9400
Domestic Relations-Child Support	473-9696
Lawyer Referral Services of Travis County Bar Assoc.	472-8303
State Bar of Texas	463-1463
Women's Advocacy Project, Inc.	477-8113

MENTAL HEALTH

Austin Child Guidance Center	451-2242
Austin Rape Crisis Center	440-7243
Assoc. for Retarded Citizens	476-7044
Child & Family Services, Inc.	478-1648
CRISIS Intervention Center	472-4357
Dayglo Family Treatment MHMR	479-6158
Juvenile Firesetter Program-Austin Fire Dept.	477-5784
MHMR - Austin-Travis County Outpatient-North	452-9571
MHMR - Austin-Travis County Outpatient-Central	476-7263
MHMR - Austin-Travis County Outpatient-East	474-2481
MHMR - Austin-Travis County Outpatient-South	447-2055
Middle Earth Resource Center	482-8336
Middle Earth Crisis Number	447-8459
Middle Earth Administration	447-5942
Morning Glory Treatment Center	251-3298
Suicide Prevention Center	472-4357
The Settlement Club Home	836-2150
Youth Advocacy Program	385-3325, 477-2809

SPECIAL ACTIVITIES

Austin Children's Museum	472-2494
Austin Community Schools	451-7426
Austin Nature Center	327-8180
Austin Public Libraries	473-4102
Austin Parks & Recreation	499-6739
Discovery Hall	474-7616
Laguna Gloria Art Museum	327-7391
Pioneer Farm	837-1215

SPECIAL NEEDS

ARCIL-Austin Resource Center for Independent Living	443-3811
Assoc. for Children & Adults with Learning Disabilities	477-5516, 451-4520
Assoc. for Retarded Citizens	476-7044
Attention Deficit-Hyperactive Disorders	346-3123, 451-4520

AISD - Early Childhood Diagnostic Center	459-8965
Austin Parks & Recreation Dept.	327-6498, 327-6683
Beep Baseball	870-3171, 443-7071
Camp Bluebonnet	322-9292
Camp-I-Can, Camp-U-Can	478-2581
Camp Sweeney	817-665-9502
CampSign	469-9891
Capital Area Easter Seals	478-2581
Capitol Bowling Center	452-2518
Coalition of Texans with Disabilities	451-2897
Commission for the Blind-Texas	459-2506
Commission for the Deaf-Texas	469-9891
CRISP -	458-2049, 258-9251
Community Resources & Information for Special People	
Extend-A-Care	454-6638
Governor's Committee for Disabled Persons	445-8276
Heartland League Rehabilitation Institute	858-4638
HELP-Handicapped Equestrian Learning Program	836-4544
Knights of Columbus Deaf Center	443-5330
Library for the Blind	463-5458
Moms of Kids with Down's Syndrome	251-9743, 251-9040
Muscular Dystrophy Assoc.	345-3800
Multiple Sclerosis Society of Austin	452-5787
National Camps for Blind Children	267-1160
Natl. Foundation March of Dimes	328-3463
Natl. Multiple Sclerosis Society	452-5787
Orton Dyslexia Society	454-1239
PATH-Partnerships in Assisting Texans with Handicaps	331-5623
Pediatric Rehabilitation Services	480-8315
Pediatric Pulmonary Clinic	459-2121, ext. 5850
Pilot Parents (Down's Syndrome)	476-7044
SKIP-Infants with long-term needs	282-5683
Texas Assoc. for Children & Adults with Learning Disabilities	458-8234
Texas Autistic Citizens Society	467-0799
Texas Human Services-Community Services for Disabled	444-0511
Texas Lions Camp	1-896-8580
Texas School for the Blind	454-8631
Texas School for the Deaf	440-5300
Texas Special Olympics	835-9873
Travis County Services for the Deaf	448-7597
United Cerebral Palsy Assoc. of Texas	472-8696
United Cerebral Palsy Assoc. of the Capital Area	474-6717
Vaughn House, Inc. (Deaf Services)	444-9763
Vocational Rehabilitation	447-0616

SUPPORT GROUPS

ACES-Assoc. for Children for Enforcement of Support, Inc.	452-0807

ALMA-Adult Adoptees & Birth Parents	442-ALMA
Asthma Support Group	480-1607
Austin Burn Survivors	282-1820, 453-8816
Austin Council on Adoptable Children	323-6201, 834-0034
Austin Preschool Mothers Club	453-1301
Compassionate Friends (for bereaved parents)	320-7615
Family Eldercare (rearing grandchildren)	450-0844
Fathers, Mothers, Grandparents	836-1314

(Parents without custody, or grandparents of children of divorced parents)

La Leche League	836-9060
Mother To Mother	331-8921
Mothers, Inc.	327-2342, 346-2175
Mothers of Twins, Inc.	328-0974
Parent Care of Austin (premature & sick infants)	331-5512
Parents Anonymous	440-8666
Parents Without Custody	343-0994
Parents Without Partners	926-5985, 458-1818
Prevention & Cesarean Birth	467-0847
Recovery Parents (from alcohol & drugs)	478-9741
Resolve of Central Texas (infertility problems)	453-2171
Second Marriages & Stepfamilies	478-4744
Sharing & Caring (newborns-six mo.)	397-4226
Single Parents Classes	478-1648
Single Parents Support Group	447-9666
Stepparents	459-4833
Toughlove	343-0130
West Austin Preschool Mothers Group	477-1513

YOUTH ORGANIZATIONS

Big Brothers & Big Sisters, Inc.	440-8811
Boy Scouts of America-Capital Area Council	926-6363
Boys Club of Austin & Travis County	444-7199
Campfire-Balcones Council	462-2777
Girl Scouts-Lone Star Council	453-7391
YMCA of Austin	476-6705
YWCA of Austin	478-9922

Subject Index

ADOPTION/FOSTER CARE
Casey Family Program, 133
ALCOHOL & DRUG ABUSE
Charter Lane Hospital,114
ATTORNEYS
Paul Morin, 150
Vika Newsom, 150

BIOFEEDBACK
Biofeedback Training Center, 155

CAMPS
Oak Hill Summer Camp, Texas Child Care
 Inc., 95
CHILD CARE
Anderson Creative Learning Centers, 32
Children's Discovery Center, 31
Children's World Learning Centers, 31
Creative World Learning Center, 32
Hyde Park Baptist Child Development
 Center, 32
Kids Playhouse Inc., 32
Oak Hill Day Care Center, Texas Child Care
 Inc., 33
Seton's Kid Care Club & Home Health Care,
 30
Toddle Inn, 33
CLOTHING/FURNITURE
Bright Beginnings, 33
Expecting the Best, 33

DENTISTS
Raymond Oukrop, DDS, 54
Albert Tate, DDS, MSD, 54
DIVORCED PARENT SERVICES
Austin Kids Xchange, 151
Moving Through, 151

FINANCIAL PLANNING
Delta Co, 37
Financial Management Professionals, Inc.,
 36
Lance Hurley, C.F.P., 37
Chris John, C.F.C., 38

HOSPITALS
Children's Hospital at Brackenridge, 29

MEDICAL DOCTORS
Allergists
Aero-Allergen, 72

Austin Regional Clinic, 72
Larry James, M.D., 72
E.N.T./Otolaryngologists
Austin Regional Clinic, 54
Eye Doctors
O.B. Jackson, M.D., 73
Lonn Bradley Lockhart, M.D., 73
J.R. Rogers, O.D., 74
Garth Weaver, O.D., 74
Family Practice
Austin Regional Clinic, 29
James R. Brown, M.D., 28
William Franklin, M.D., 28
George Smith, M.D., 27
Allen Sonstein, M.D., 27
Southwest Family Practice, 28
Andrew Weary, M.D., 29
Obstetrics/Gynecology
Mark Akin, M.D., 129
Austin Regional Clinic, 131
Robert Casanova, M.D., 128
Vernon Elledge, M.D., 130
Patricia Gunter, M.D., 130
Jo Bess Hammer, M.D., 128
Joe McIlhaney, Jr., M.D., 131
Cindy Mingea, M.D., 130
Christopher Seeker, M.D., 131
Emilio Torres, M.D., 131
Jeffrey Youngkin, M.D., 129
Pediatricians
Austin Regional Clinic, 26
Plastic Surgeons
David Wishnew, M.D., 55
Psychiatrists
Austin Regional Clinic, 113
Charter Lane Hospital, 95, 114
Marlowe Helen Donaldson, M.D., 153
James Maynard, M.D., 114
Cathey Roberts, M.D., 154
St. David's Adolescent Psychiatric Day
 Hospital, 112
MENTAL HEALTH
Licensed Professional Counselors
Central Texas Counseling & Family
 Therapy, 94, 112
Kay G. Hibbs, 94
Michael J. Sliwa, 112
Psychologists
Kathleen Adams, Ph.D., 95
Austin Regional Clinic, 113
Connie Benfield, Ph.D., 113

To order additional books, send $6.95 plus $2.00 tax, shipping & handling to:

CAMERON PUBLICATIONS
P.O. Box 3493
Austin, Texas 78764
Discounts available for bulk orders.

by Joseph Manor, grade 8, Lamar Middle School